MAZE !

Draw a line from start to exit.

start

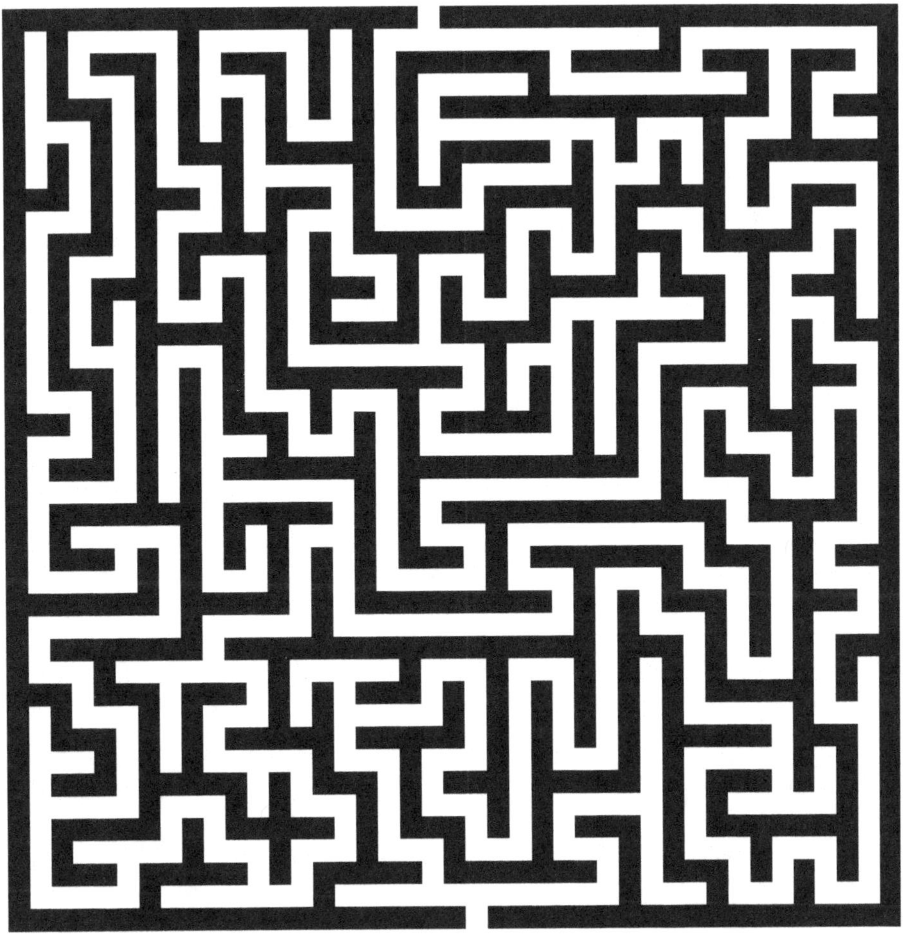

exit

DRAW THE FACES

Continue drawing the faces below.

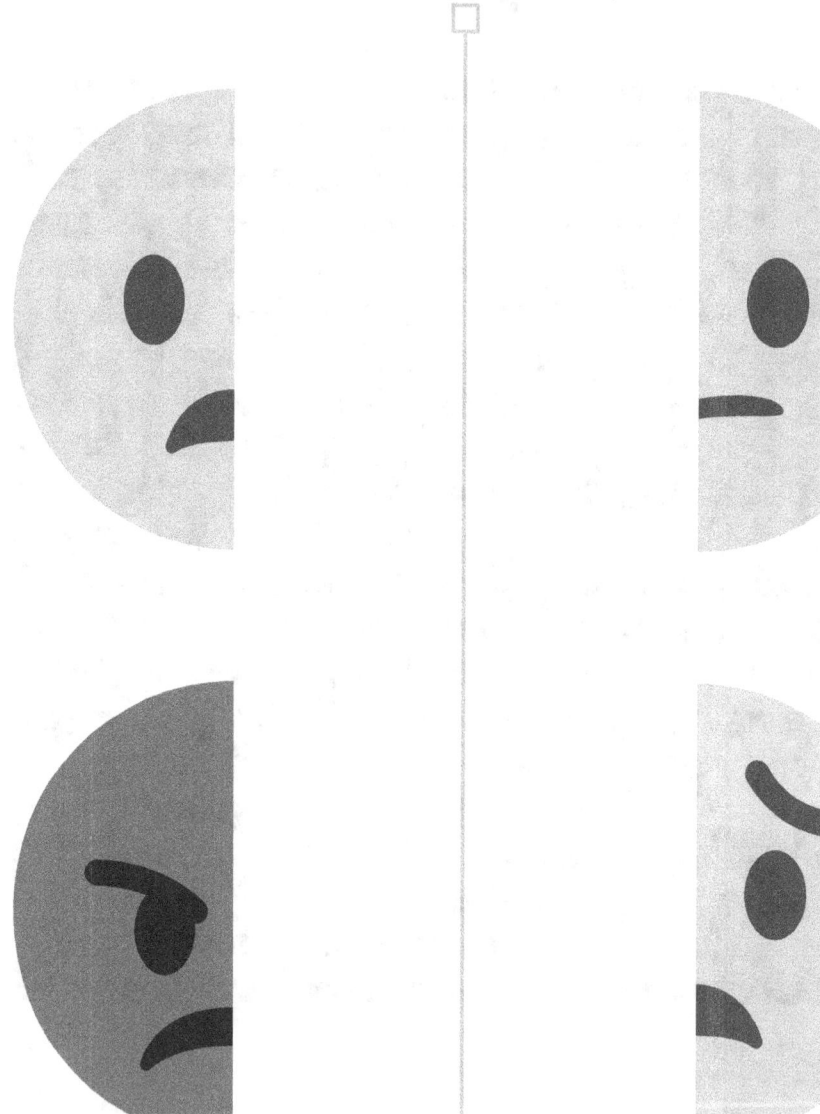

Mrs. Red's Fruit Stand

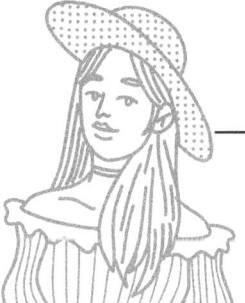

8

Mrs. Red sells fruit in boxes of
Make sure each box has eight by drawing the missing fruits.

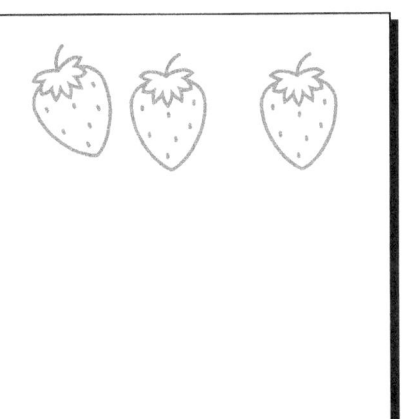

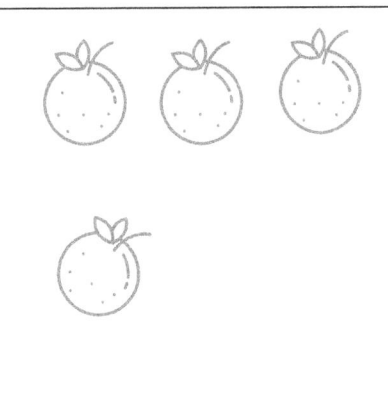

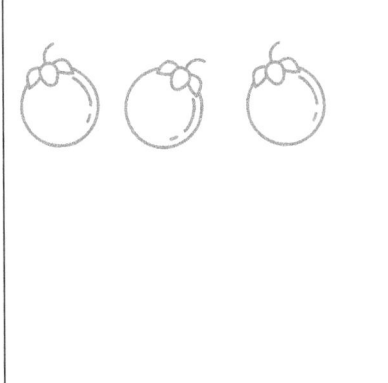

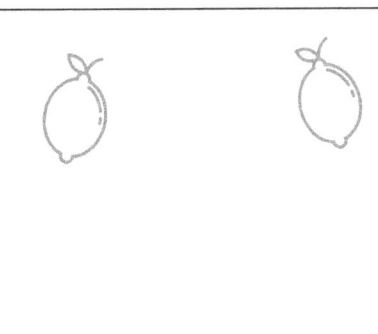

ALL ABOUT SHAPES

Trace and color in the shapes below.

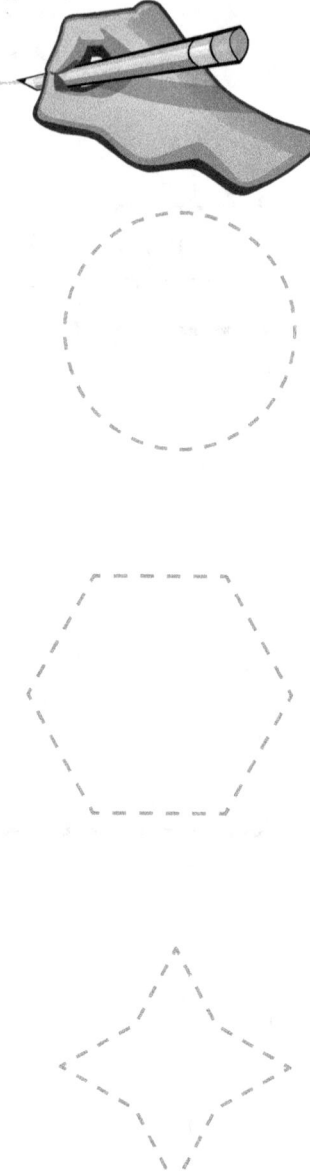

WHAT TIME IS IT?

Read the time from the digital clocks
**Can you set the correct time on the analog
clocks by drawing the correct hands?**

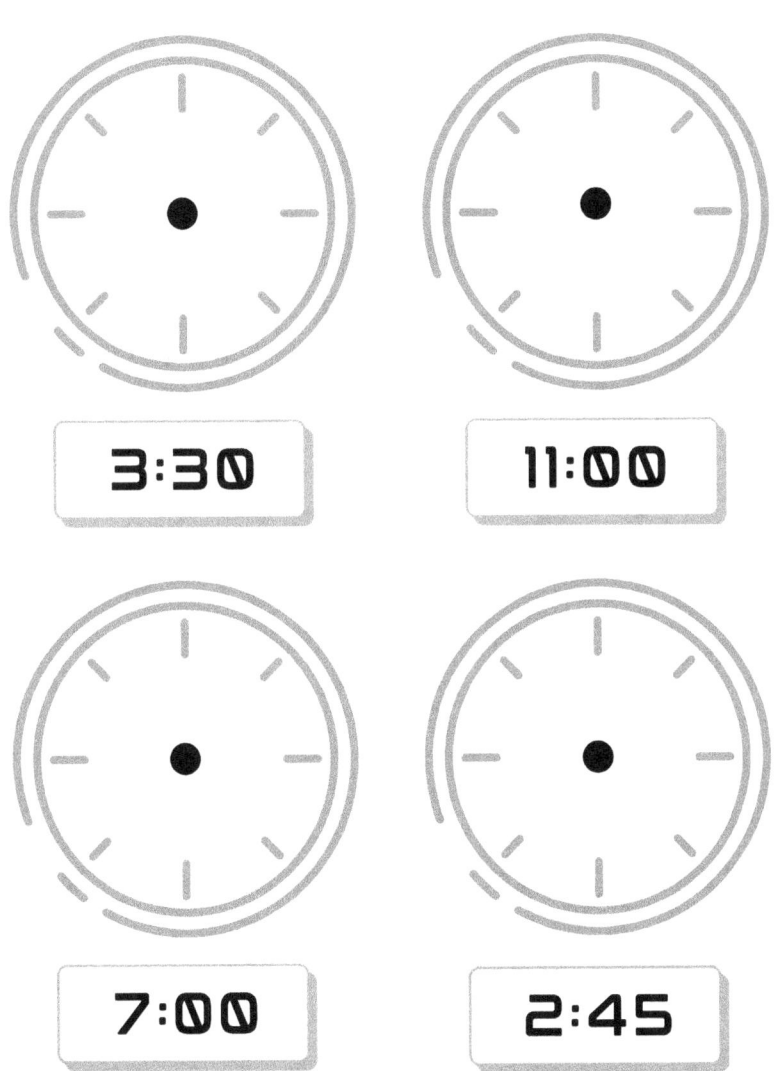

PRINTS AND PATTERNS

Using the different materials you brought, create a unique pattern for each drawing below. Combine geometric and organic shapes to make your patterns.

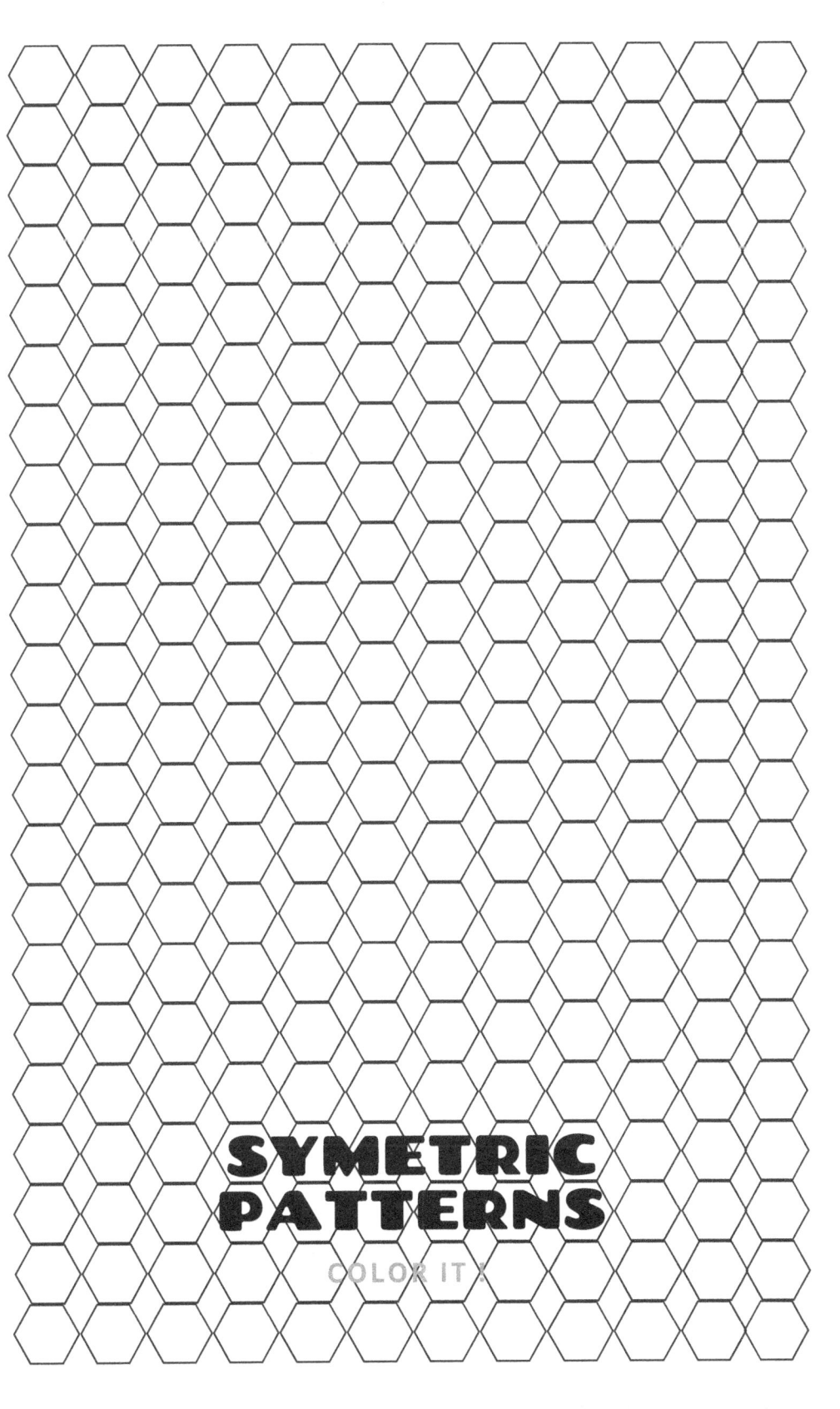

SYMETRIC PATTERNS

COLOR IT !

4 IN A ROW

Each turn each player puts a piece of his color inside a column and it will fall until it reaches the lowest available spot.
The one who can put 4 pieces of the same color in a row horizontally, vertically or diagonally wins.

PLAYER 1 : _____

PLAYER 2 : _____

WHO WINS ? : _____

Mrs. Green's Fruit Stand

7

Mrs. Green sells fruit in boxes of
Make sure each box has seven by drawing the missing fruits.

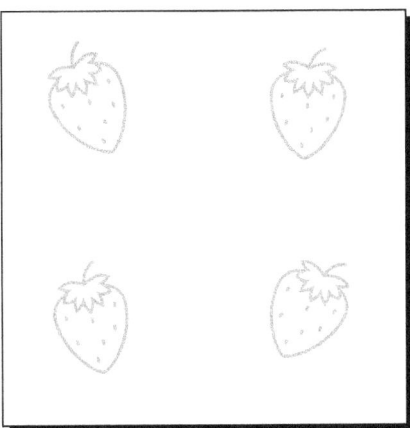

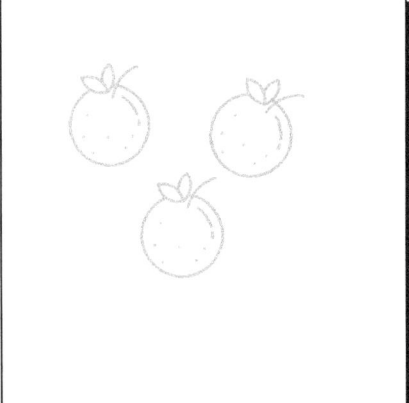

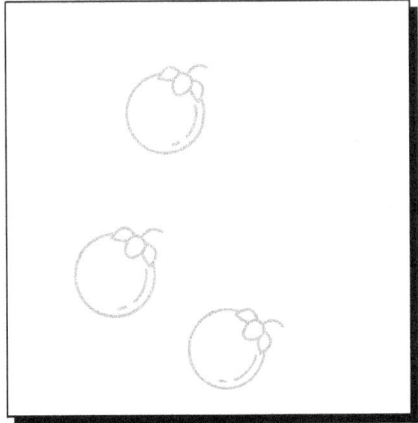

round 1

round 2

round 3

round 4

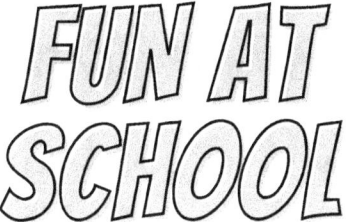

FUN AT SCHOOL

In the box, draw and color your favorite thing about school.

In school, I like _____

because _____

_____

_____

_____

FUN WITH FRACTIONS

LEARN HOW TO ADD AND SUBTRACT FRACTIONS!

Write down the fraction indicated by each drawing in each row then write down the answer to the problem.

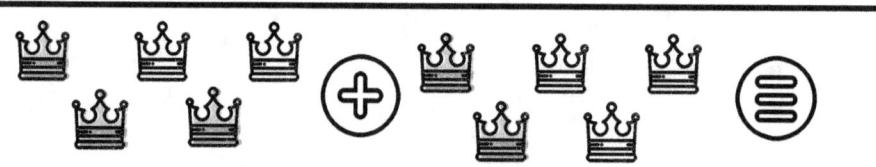

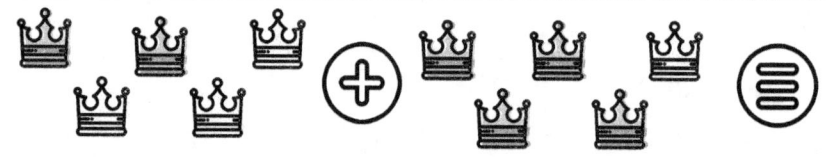

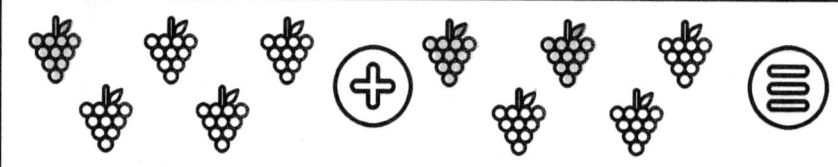

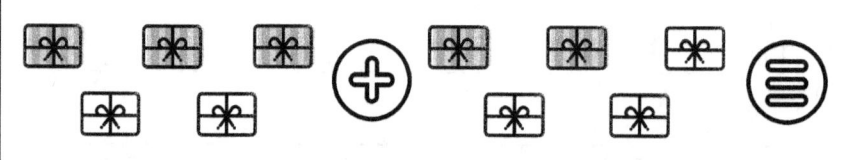

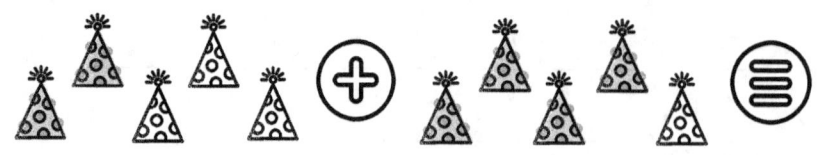

MISSING PARTS

Draw a line to the missing part.

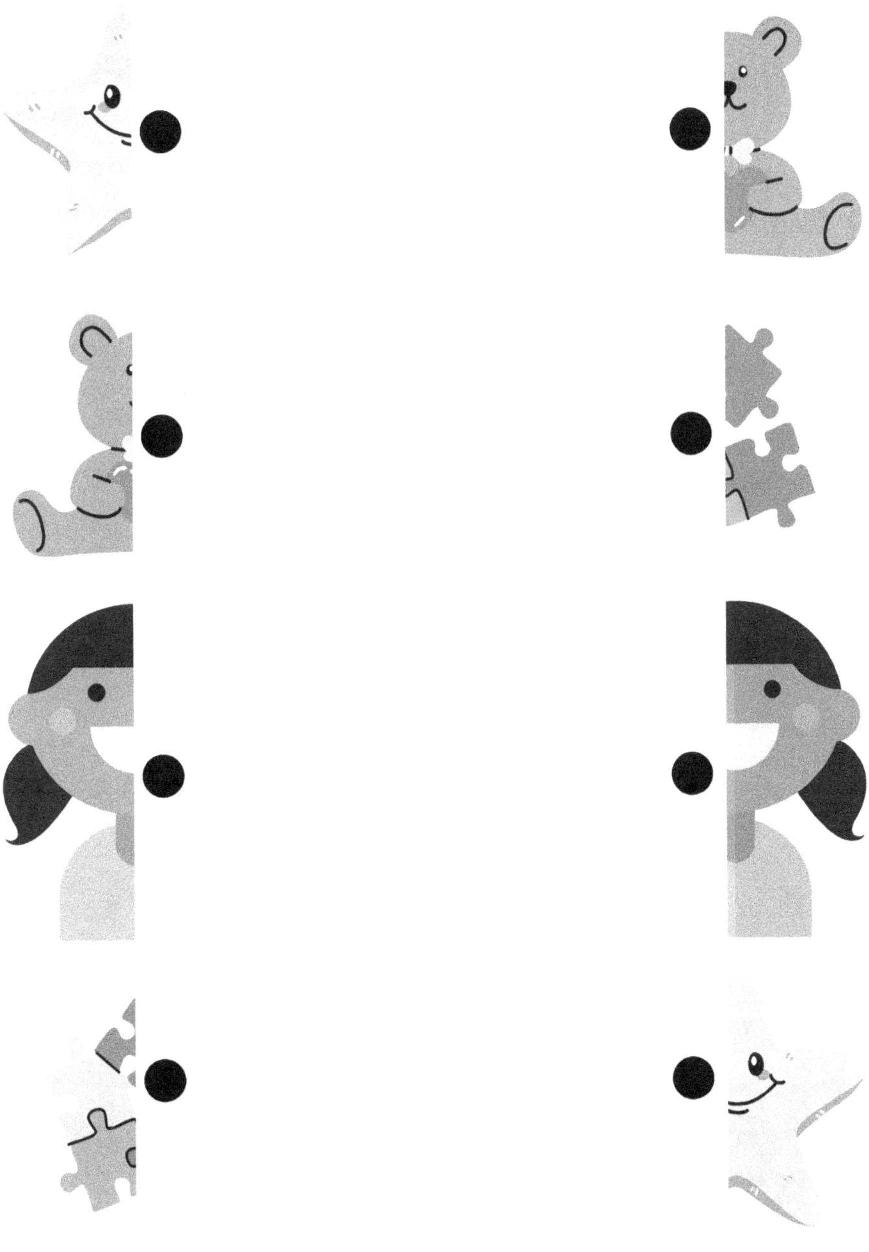

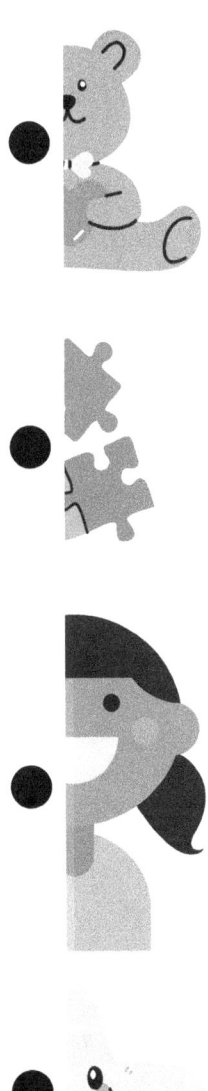

LET'S GO TO THE GARDEN AND DRAW!

Instructions:
In this garden, you'll find lots of leaves. Choose one and copy it by drawing and coloring.
Have fun!

Mrs. Green's Fruit Stand

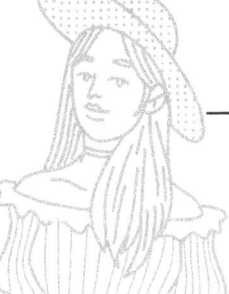

Mrs. Green sells fruit in boxes of 2
Make sure each box has two by drawing the missing fruits.

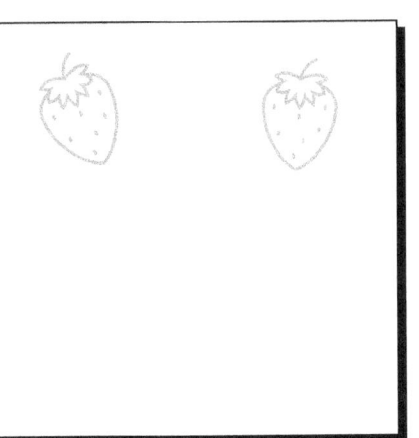

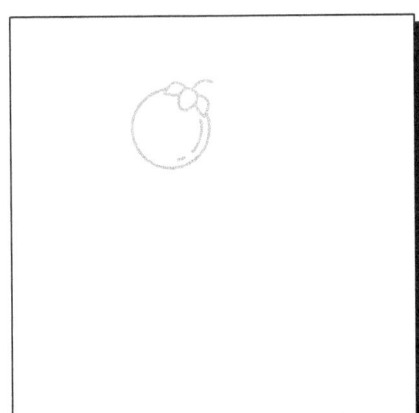

POP ART GRID CHALLENGE

Print out 1 artwork by either Andy Warhol, Roy Lichtenstein, or Keith Haring. Draw a 5x5 grid on your photo. Using the materials you have, try to recreate the piece on the grid below by drawing one square at a time.

MAZE !

Draw a line from start to exit.

start

exit

LINE ART

Demonstrate your mastery of geometric elements by creating an illustration using them! Use colored markers to identify them using the coloring key below.

COLORING KEY:

○ right angles ○ points ● obtuse angles ○ rays

○ acute angles ● lines ● line segments

WHO AM I?

Use the space below to draw a self-portrait. On the left side, draw how you look on the outside. On the right side, draw your favorite toys, animals, food, or games. Color your creation when you're done!

Materials:
Pencil, Crayons

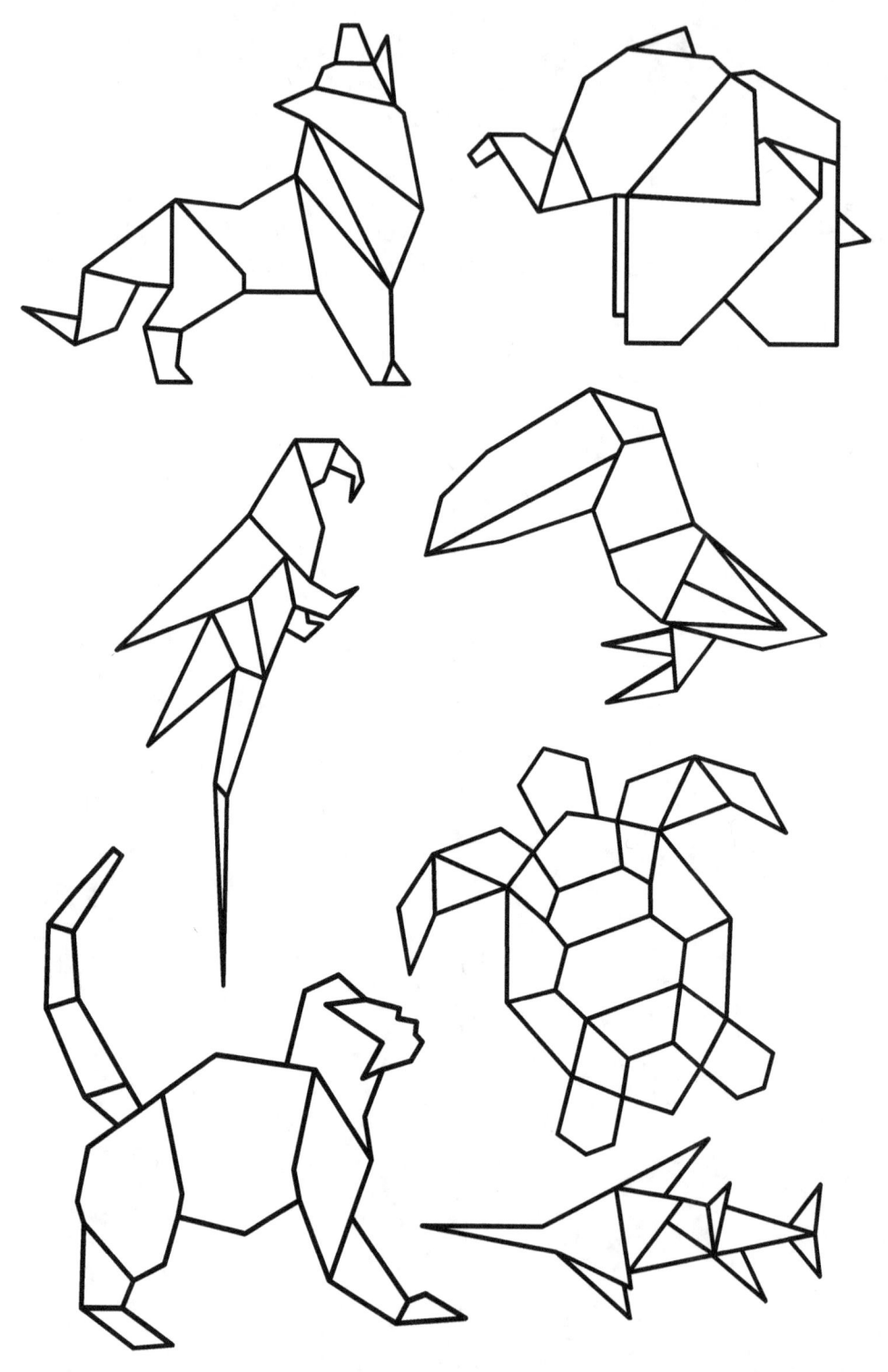

Mrs. Red's Fruit Stand

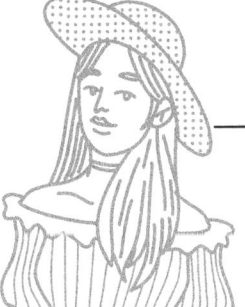

5

Mrs. Red sells fruit in boxes of
Make sure each box has five by drawing the missing fruits.

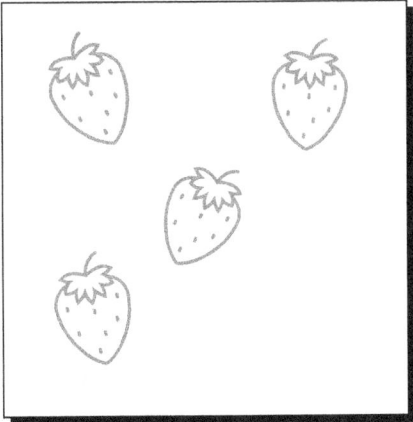

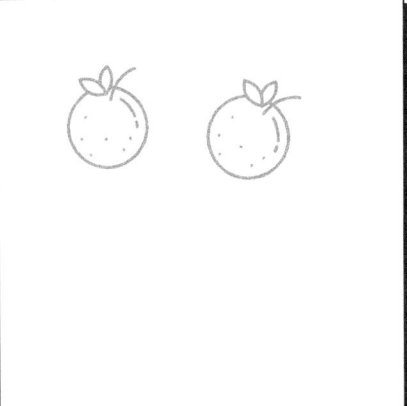

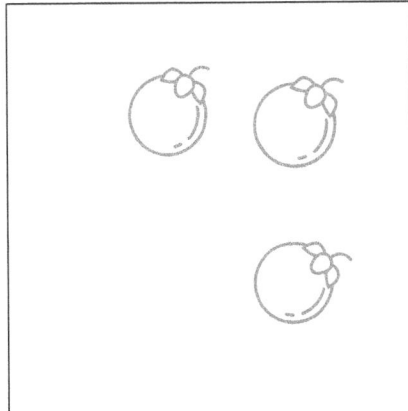

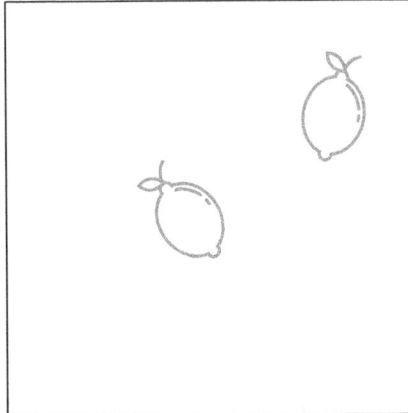

MISSING DOTS

Complete the equation by drawing the missing dots.

$\boxed{\raisebox{0pt}{·· }} + \boxed{} = 8$ $\boxed{\raisebox{0pt}{:: }} + \boxed{} = 5$

$\boxed{} + \boxed{\raisebox{0pt}{··· }} = 8$ $\boxed{} + \boxed{\raisebox{0pt}{::: }} = 7$

$\boxed{\raisebox{0pt}{· }} + \boxed{} = 4$ $\boxed{\raisebox{0pt}{··· }} + \boxed{} = 6$

$\boxed{} + \boxed{\raisebox{0pt}{··· }} = 3$ $\boxed{} + \boxed{\raisebox{0pt}{··· }} = 8$

$\boxed{\raisebox{0pt}{· }} + \boxed{} = 2$ $\boxed{\raisebox{0pt}{:: }} + \boxed{} = 9$

$\boxed{} + \boxed{\raisebox{0pt}{· }} = 3$ $\boxed{} + \boxed{\raisebox{0pt}{··· }} = 4$

IT'S MONKEY TIME!

Help Monkey Set His Alarm

Instructions: Monkey follows a schedule for his daily tasks. Help him set his alarm by drawing the arms on the clock.

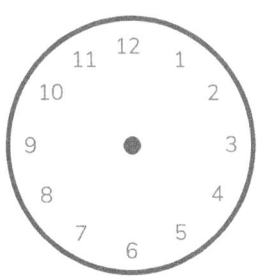

WAKE UP, MONKEY! 6:30AM

EAT LUNCH, MONKEY! 11:30AM

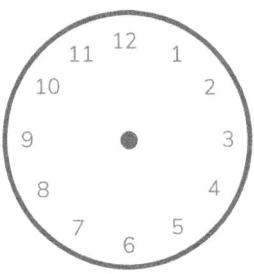

PLAY OUTSIDE, MONKEY! 4:00PM

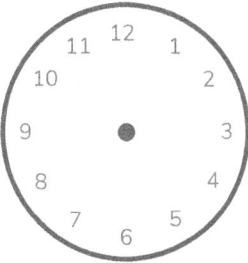

GO TO BED, MONKEY! 8:00 PM

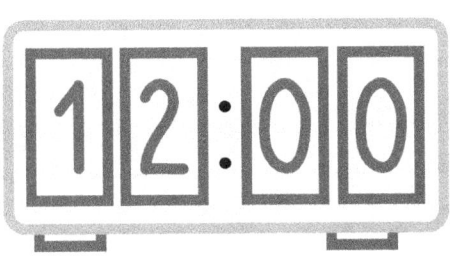

DRAW THE FACES

Continue drawing the faces below.

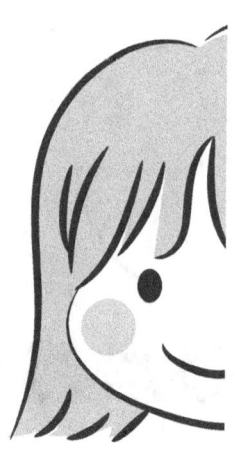

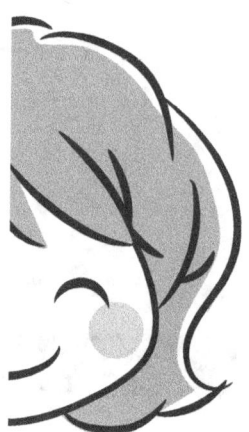

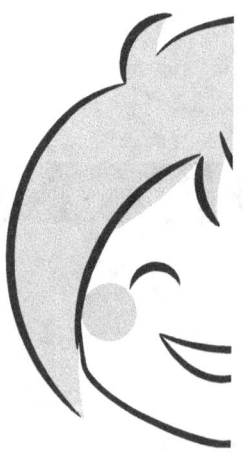

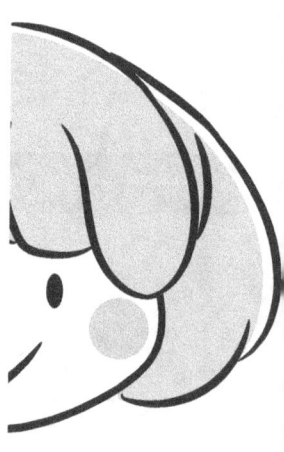

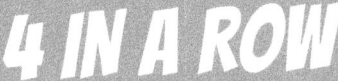 4 IN A ROW

Each turn each player puts a piece of his color inside a column and it will fall until it reaches the lowest available spot. The one who can put 4 pieces of the same color in a row horizontally, vertically or diagonally wins.

PLAYER 1 : _____

PLAYER 2 : _____

WHO WINS ? : _____

Mrs. Green's Fruit Stand

6

Mrs. Green sells fruit in boxes of
Make sure each box has six by drawing the missing fruits.

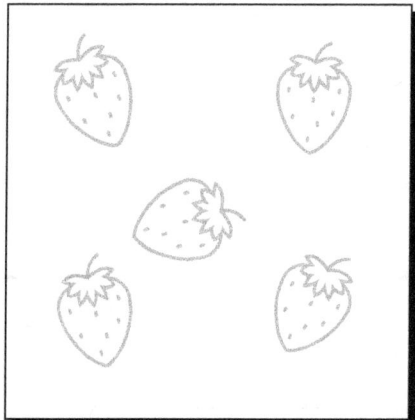

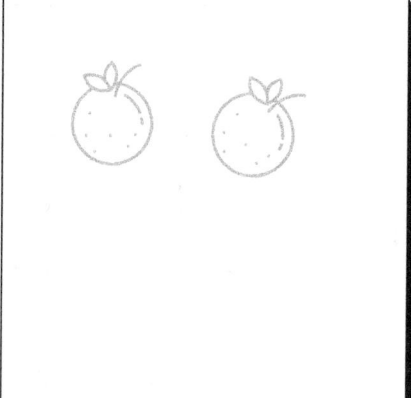

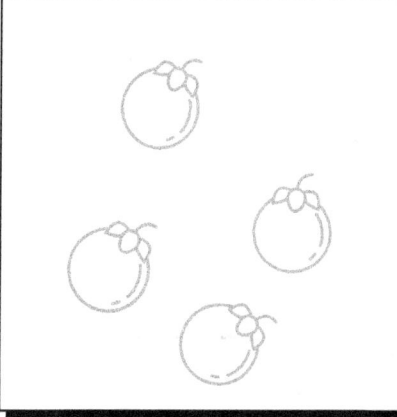

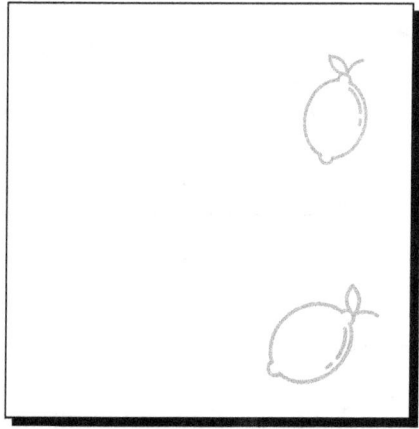

FUN AT SCHOOL

In the box, draw and color your favorite thing about school.

In school, I like _____

_____

because _____

_____

_____

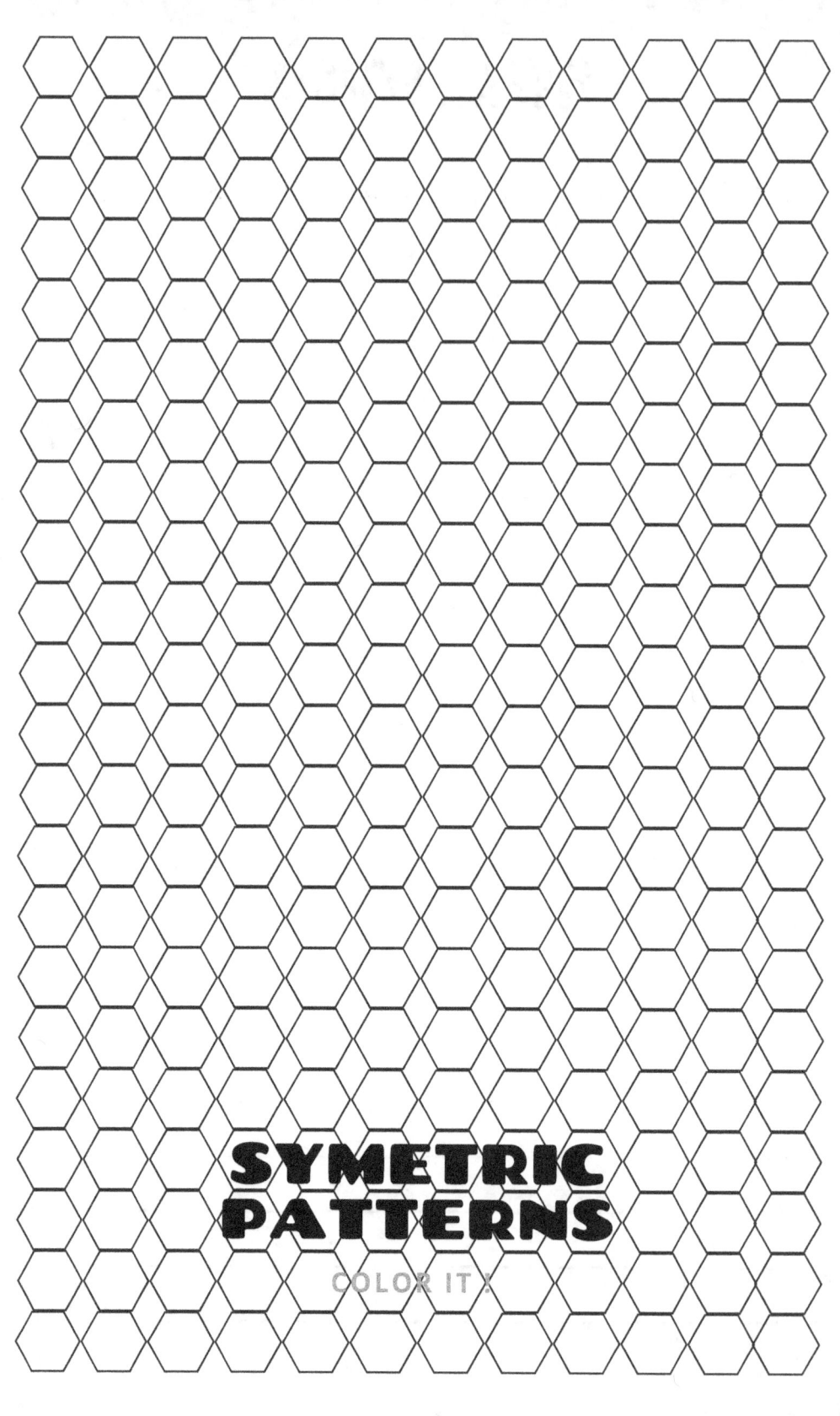

SYMETRIC
PATTERNS

COLOR IT !

LINE ART

Demonstrate your mastery of geometric elements by creating an illustration using them! Use colored markers to identify them using the coloring key below.

COLORING
KEY:
- ⬤ right angles
- ⬤ acute angles
- ⬤ points
- ⬤ lines
- ⬤ obtuse angles
- ⬤ line segments
- ⬤ rays

MAZE !

Draw a line from start to exit.

start

exit

Mrs. Red's Fruit Stand

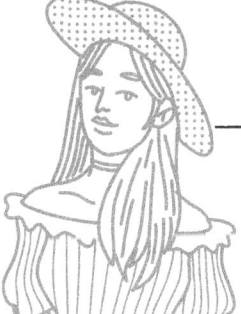

Mrs. Red sells fruit in boxes of **4**
Make sure each box has four by drawing the missing fruits.

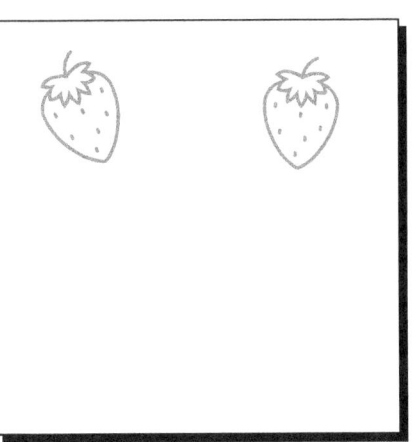

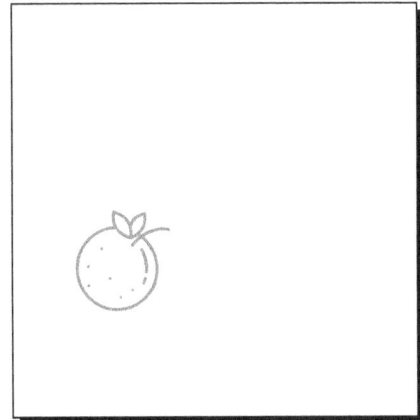

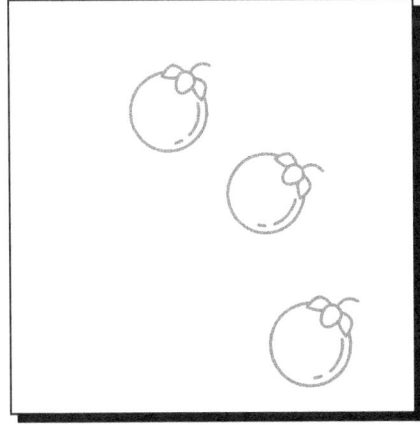

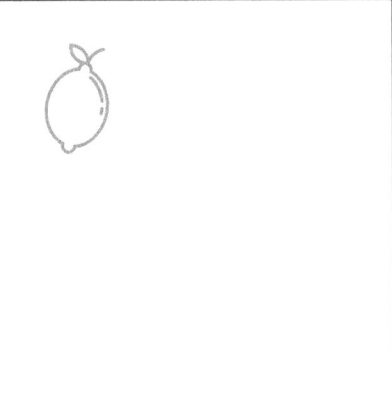

LINE ART

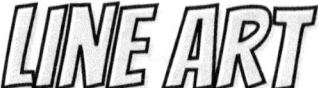

Demonstrate your mastery of geometric elements by creating an illustration using them! Use colored markers to identify them using the coloring key to the right.

COLORING KEY

- points
- rays
- right angles
- line segments
- acute angles
- obtuse angles
- lines

MISSING DOTS

Complete the equation by drawing the missing dots.

[2] + [ ] = 5

[4] + [ ] = 9

[ ] + [3] = 7

[ ] + [6] = 8

[1] + [ ] = 6

[3] + [ ] = 4

[ ] + [2] = 8

[ ] + [5] = 7

[1] + [ ] = 3

[4] + [ ] = 5

[ ] + [1] = 2

[ ] + [3] = 6

POP ART GRID CHALLENGE

Print out 1 artwork by either Andy Warhol, Roy Lichtenstein, or Keith Haring. Draw a 5x5 grid on your photo. Using the materials you have, try to recreate the piece on the grid below by drawing one square at a time.

Mrs. Green's Fruit Stand

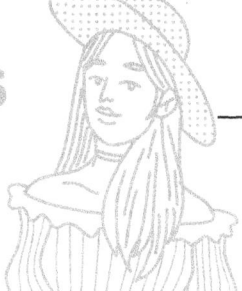

Mrs. Green sells fruit in boxes of **8**
Make sure each box has eight by drawing the missing fruits.

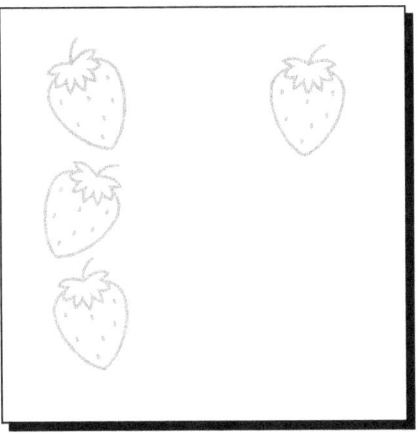

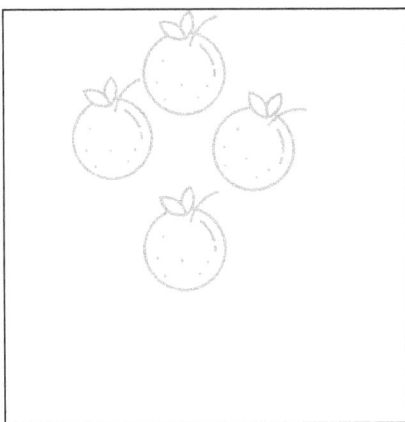

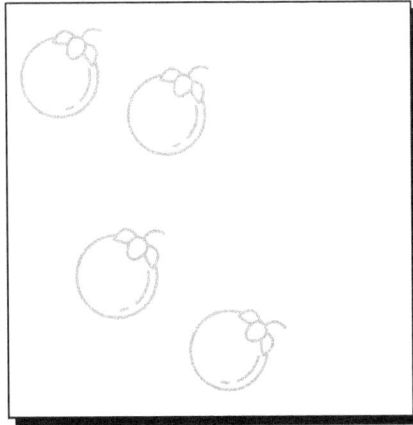

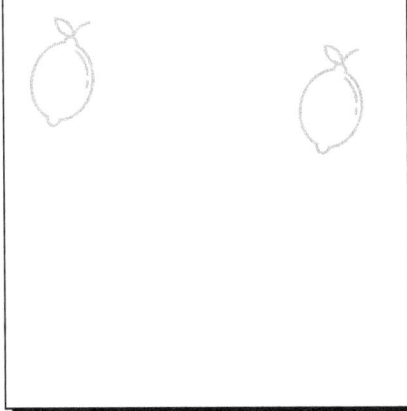

round 1

round 2

round 3

round 4

DRAW THE SHAPES

Continue drawing the shapes below.

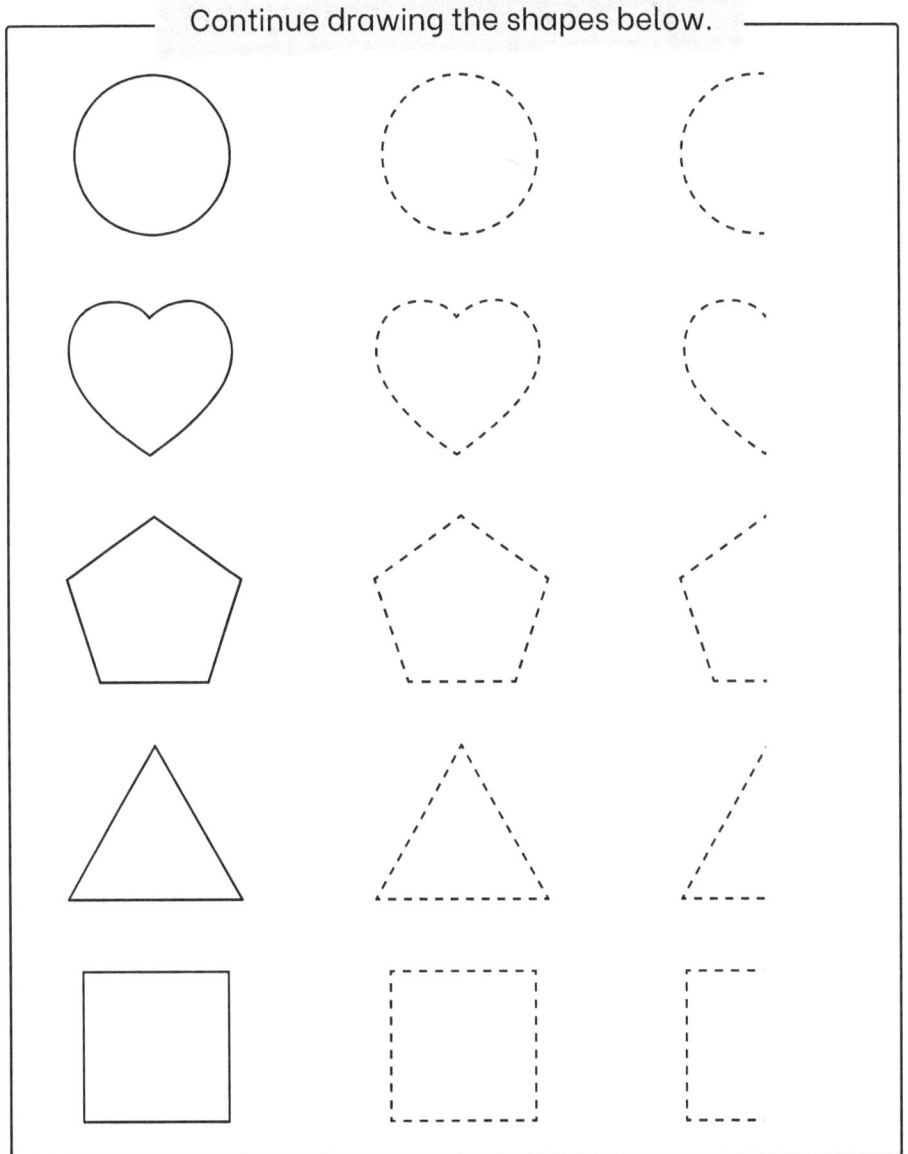

WHAT TIME IS IT?

Read the time from the digital clocks.
Can you set the correct time on the analog clocks by drawing the correct hands?

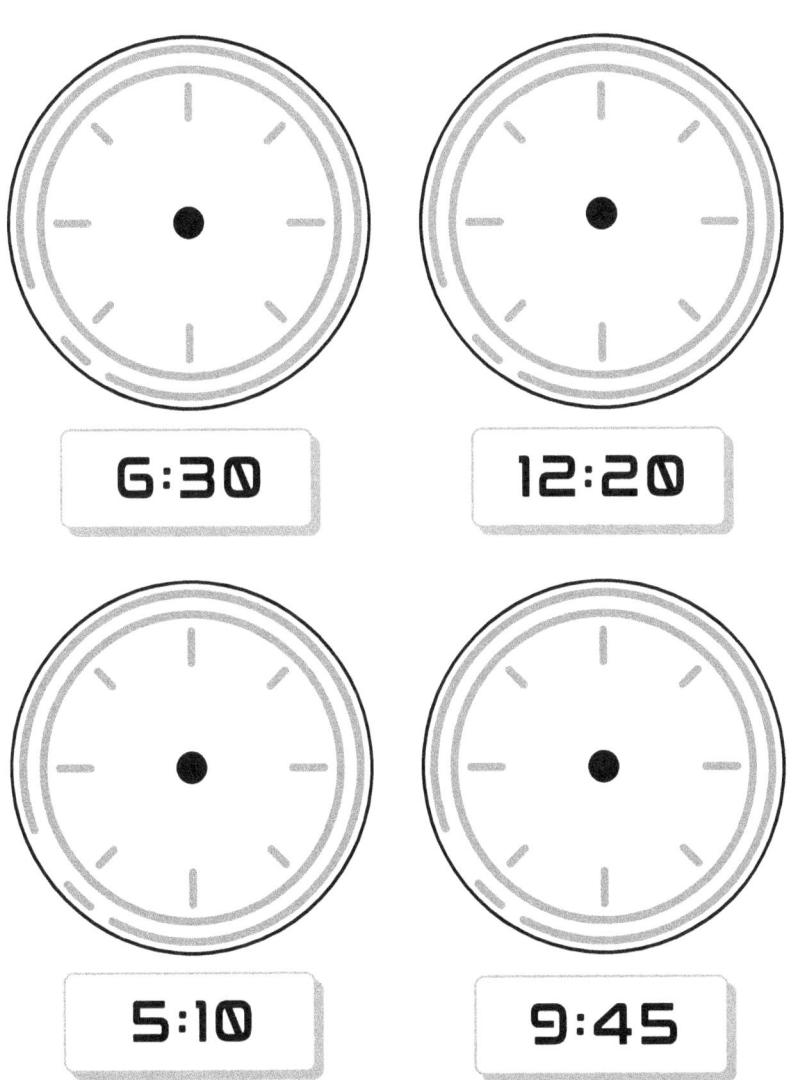

6:30

12:20

5:10

9:45

Mrs. Red's Fruit Stand

3

Mrs. Red sells fruit in boxes of
Make sure each box has three by drawing the missing fruits.

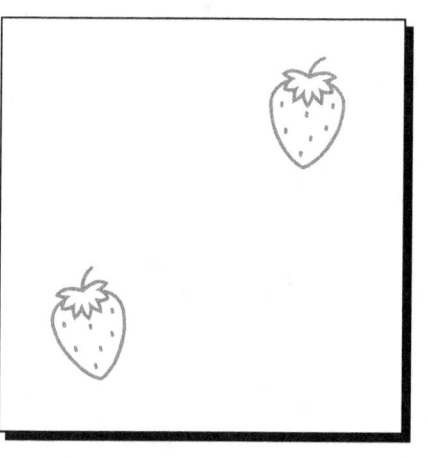

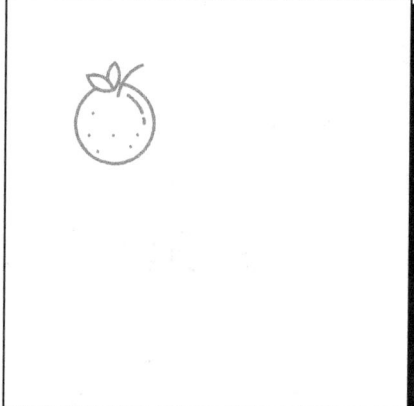

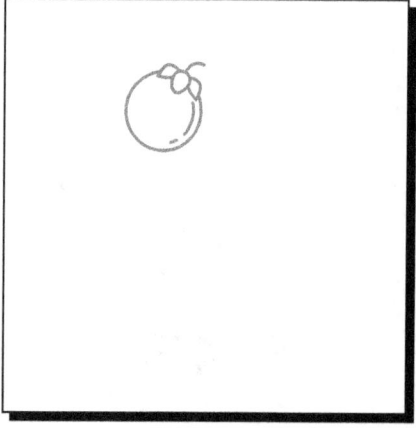

LET'S GO TO THE GARDEN AND DRAW!

Instructions:
In this garden, you'll find many trees. Choose one and copy it by drawing and coloring.
Have fun!

MAZE !

Draw a line from start to exit.

start

exit

MISSING PARTS

Draw a line to the missing part.

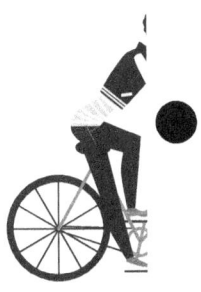
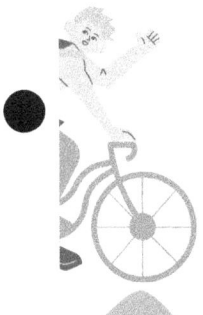
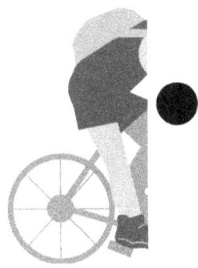
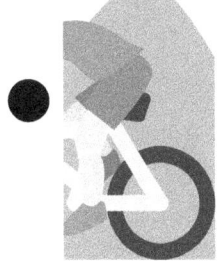
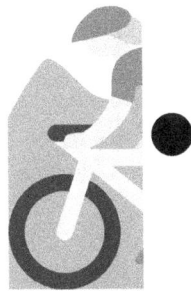
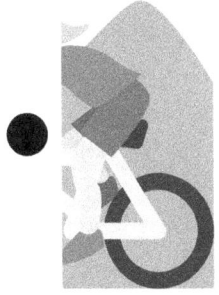
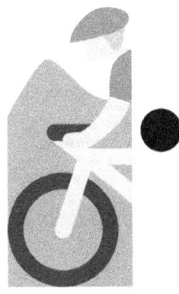
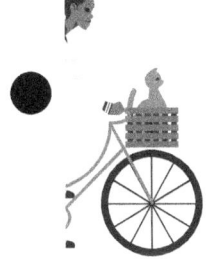

WHO IS HE?

Use the space below to draw a portrait of your friend. On the left side, draw how your friend looks on the outside. On the right side, draw his favorite toys, animals, food, or games. Color your creation when you're done!

Materials:
Pencil, Crayons

4 IN A ROW

Each turn each player puts a piece of his color inside a column and it will fall until it reaches the lowest available spot. The one who can put 4 pieces of the same color in a row horizontally, vertically or diagonally wins.

PLAYER 1 : _____

PLAYER 2 : _____

WHO WINS ? : _____

Mrs. Green's Fruit Stand

Mrs. Green sells fruit in boxes of **4**
Make sure each box has four by drawing the missing fruits.

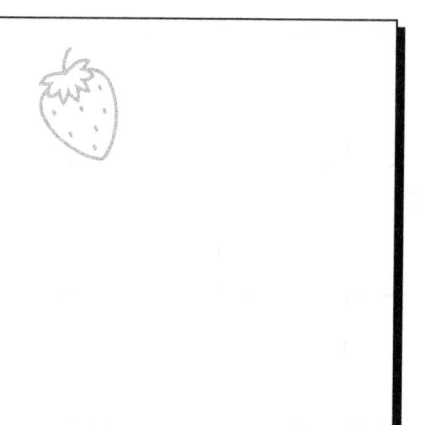

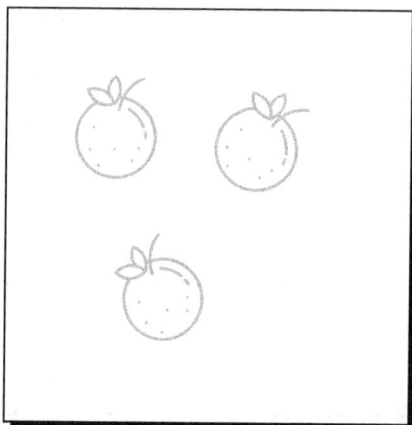

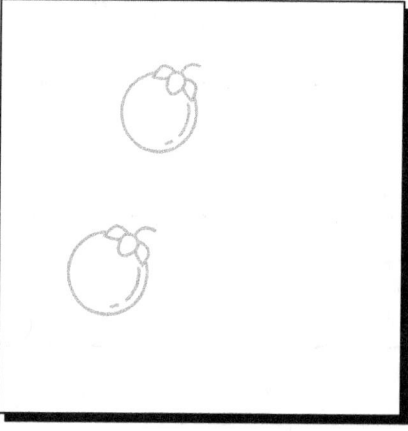

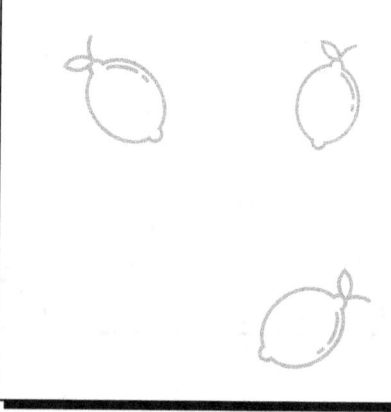

FUN WITH FRACTIONS

LEARN HOW TO ADD AND SUBTRACT FRACTIONS!

Write down the fraction indicated by each drawing in each row then write down the answer to the problem.

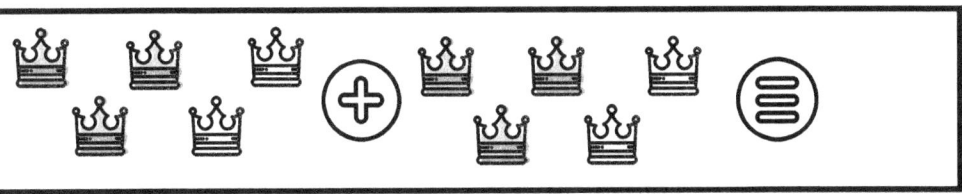

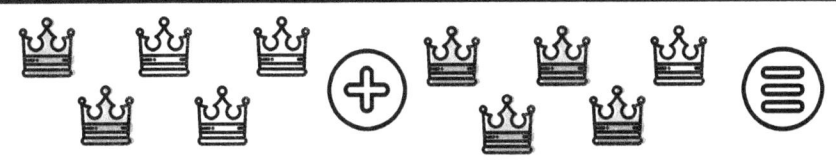

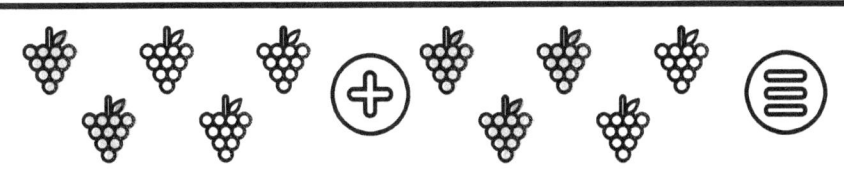

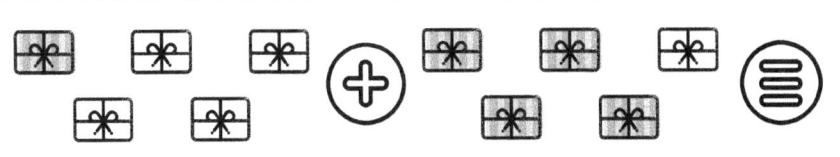

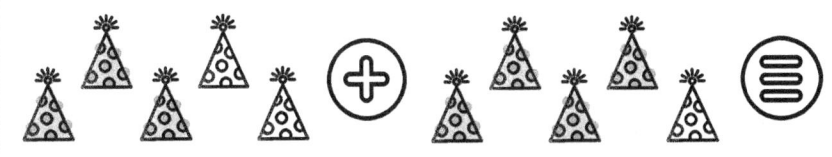

FUN AT SCHOOL

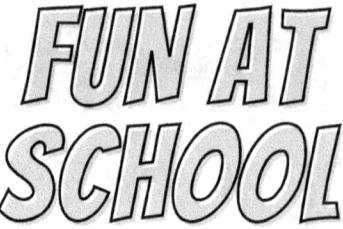
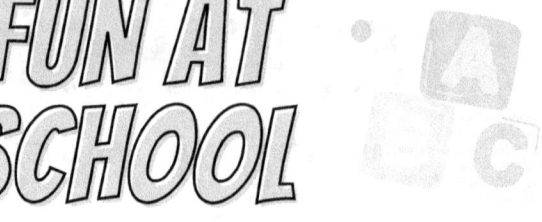

In the box, draw and color your favorite thing about school.

In school, I like _____

because _____

_____

_____

_____

_____

DRAW THE FACES

Continue drawing the faces below.

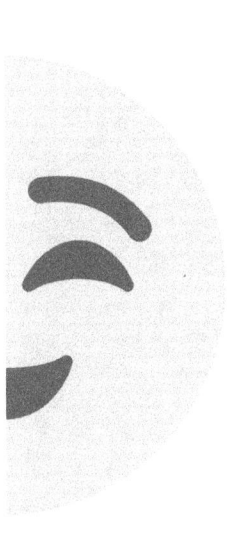
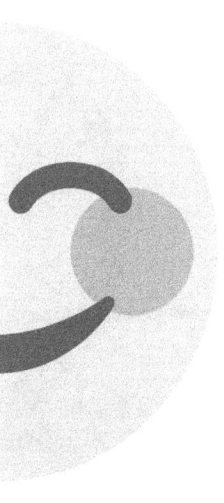

Mrs. Red's Fruit Stand

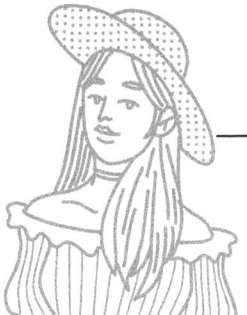

6

Mrs. Red sells fruit in boxes of
Make sure each box has six by drawing the missing fruits.

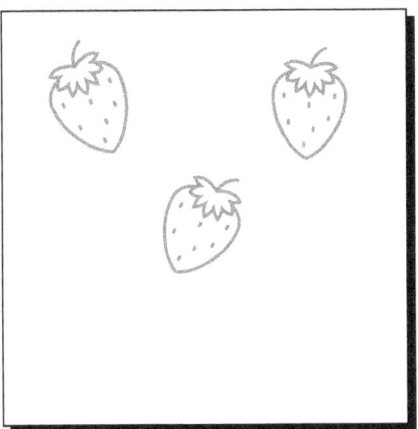

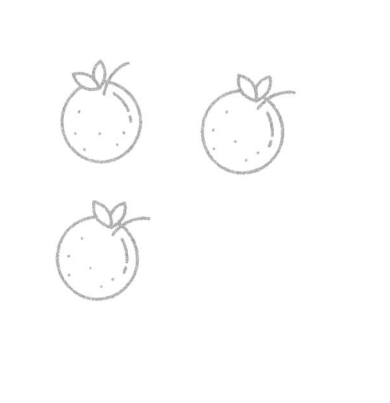

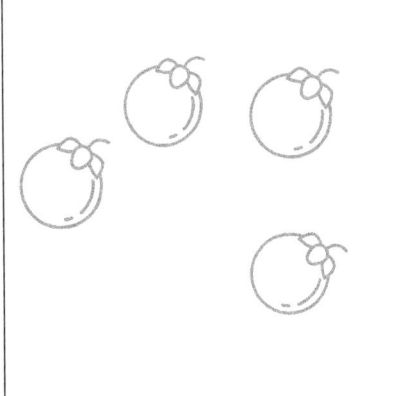

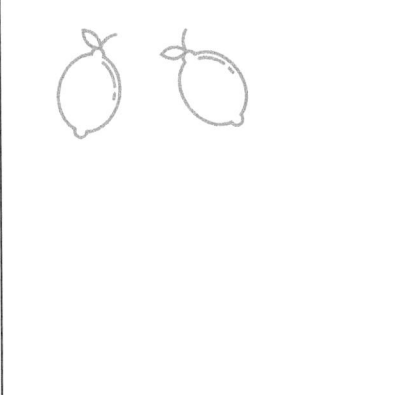

MISSING DOTS

Complete the equation by drawing the missing dots.

$\boxed{\because} + \boxed{} = 3$ $\boxed{\vcenter{\hbox{::}}} + \boxed{} = 5$

$\boxed{} + \boxed{\therefore} = 8$ $\boxed{} + \boxed{\vcenter{\hbox{:::}}} = 7$

$\boxed{\cdot} + \boxed{} = 4$ $\boxed{\therefore} + \boxed{} = 6$

$\boxed{} + \boxed{\because} = 3$ $\boxed{} + \boxed{\vcenter{\hbox{::}}} = 8$

$\boxed{\cdot} + \boxed{} = 2$ $\boxed{\vcenter{\hbox{::}}} + \boxed{} = 9$

$\boxed{} + \boxed{\cdot} = 3$ $\boxed{} + \boxed{\therefore} = 4$

MAZE !

Draw a line from start to exit.

start

exit

FLOWERS !

Using the different materials you brought, create a unique pattern
for each flower below.

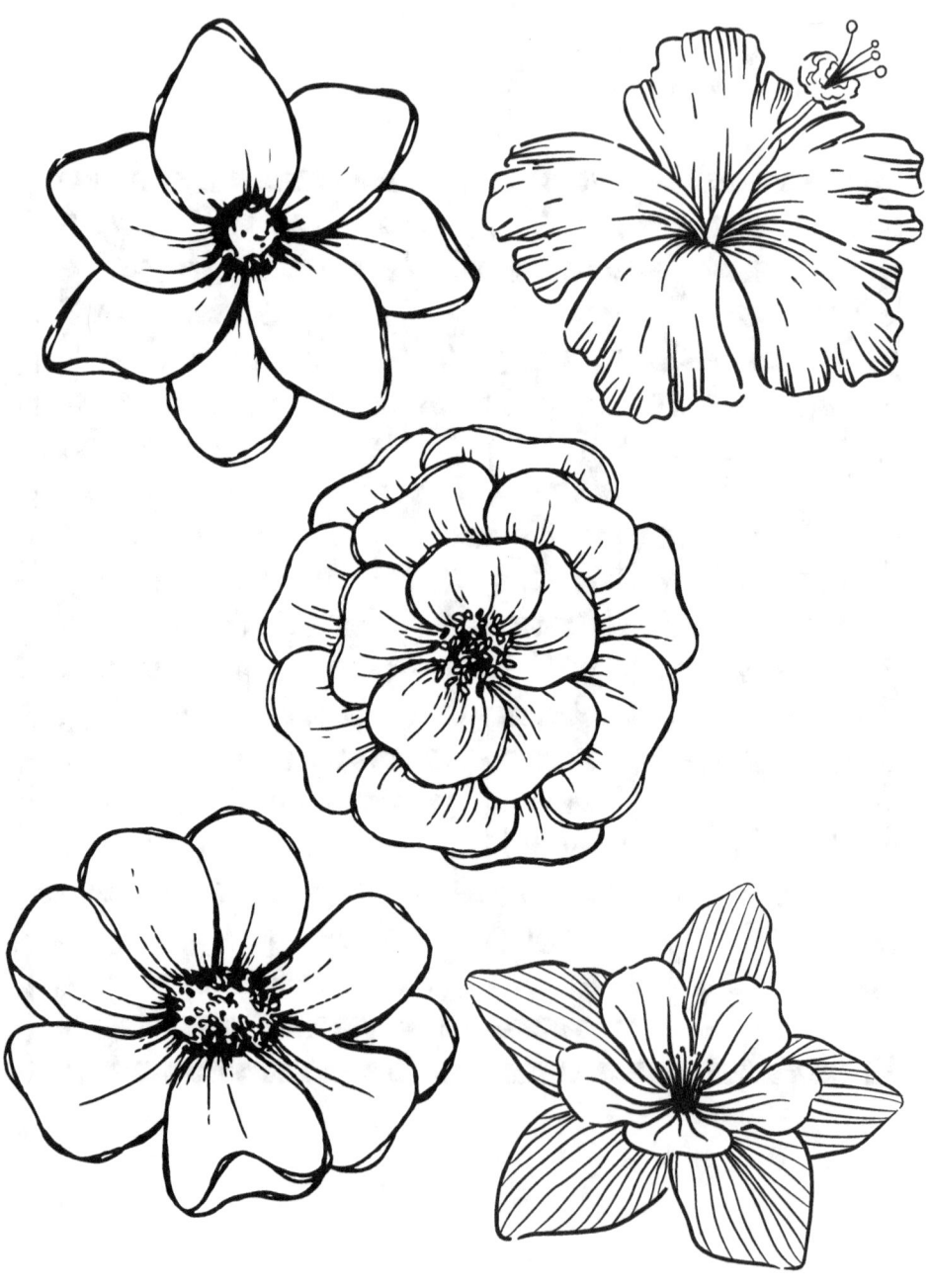

POP ART GRID CHALLENGE

Print out 1 artwork by either Andy Warhol, Roy Lichtenstein, or Keith Haring. Draw a 5x5 grid on your photo. Using the materials you have, try to recreate the piece on the grid below by drawing one square at a time.

FUN AT SCHOOL

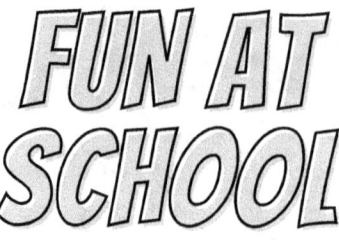

In the box, draw and color your favorite thing about school.

In school, I like _____

because _____

_____

_____

_____

ALL ABOUT SHAPES

Trace and color in the shapes below.

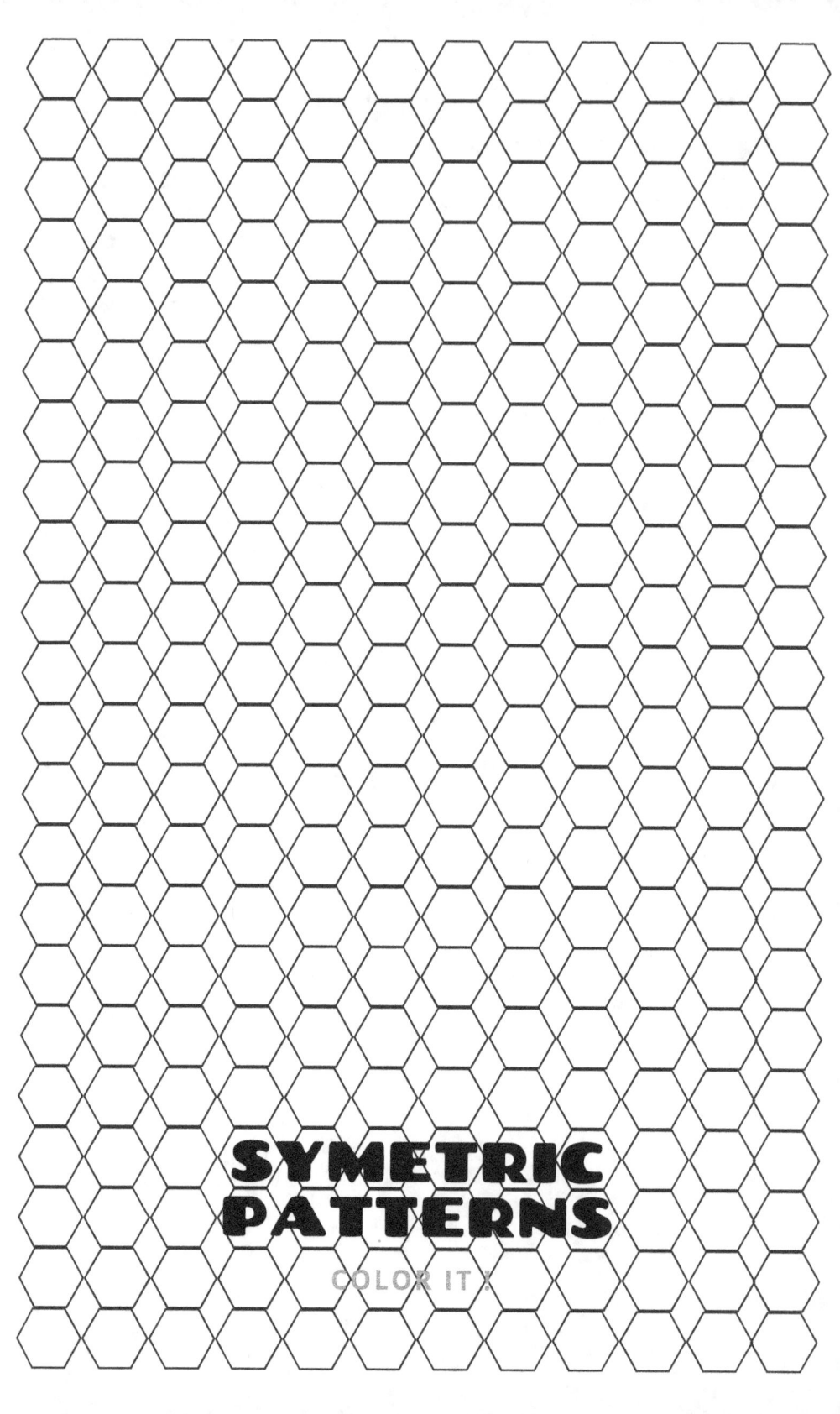

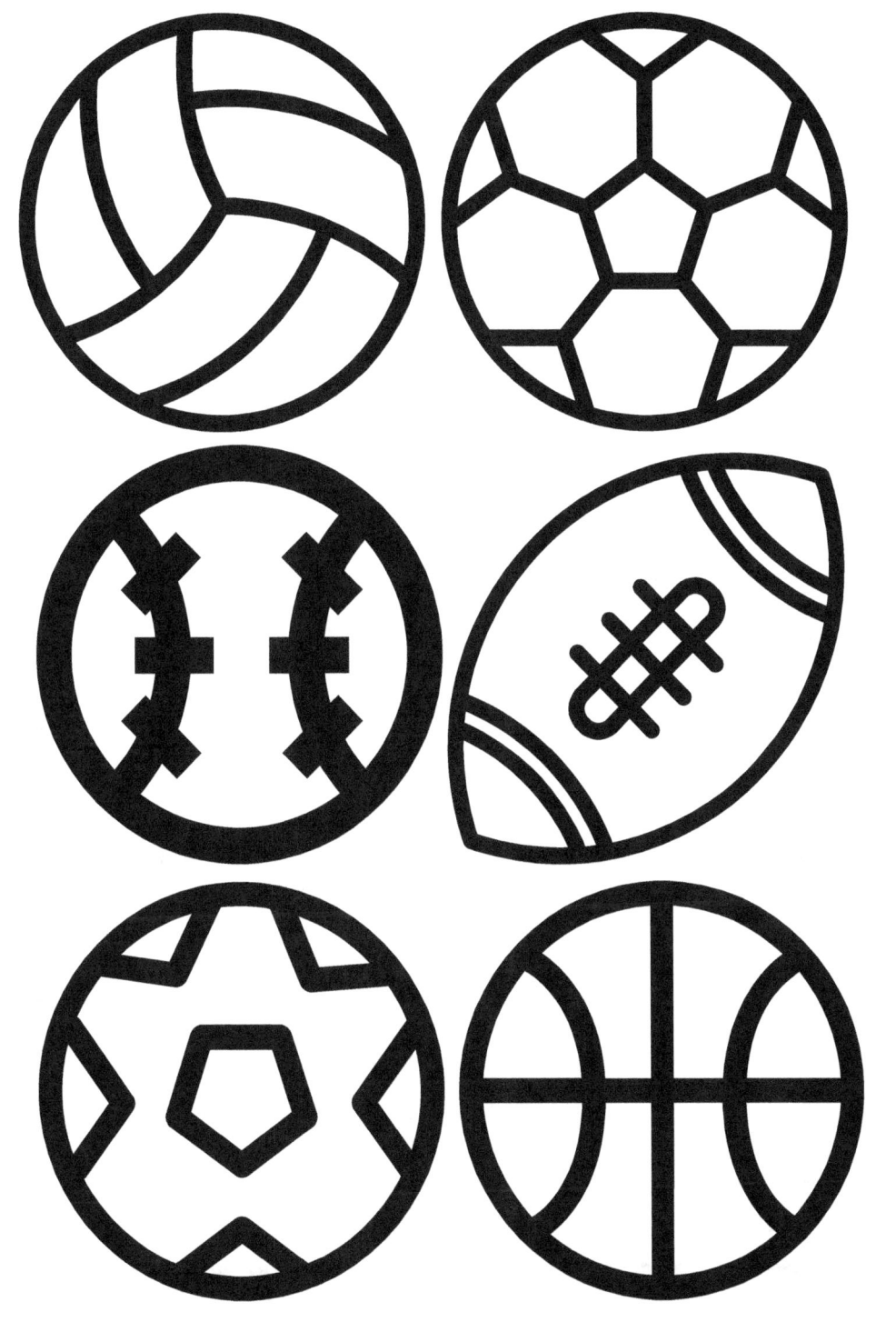

Mrs. Green's Fruit Stand

9

Mrs. Green sells fruit in boxes of
Make sure each box has nine by drawing the missing fruits.

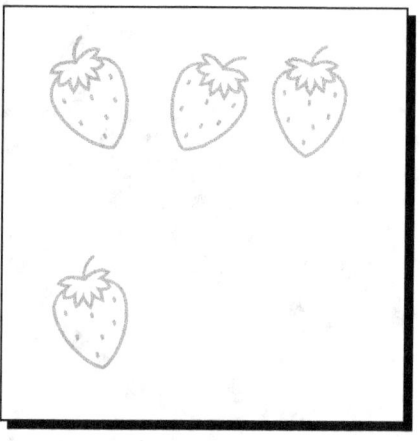

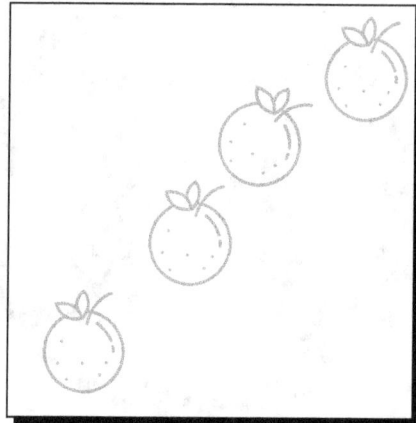

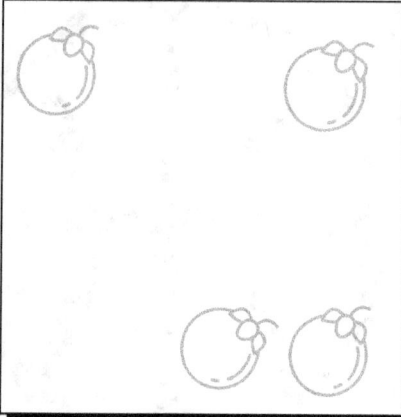

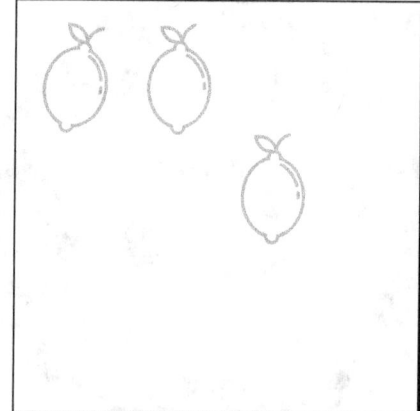

round 1

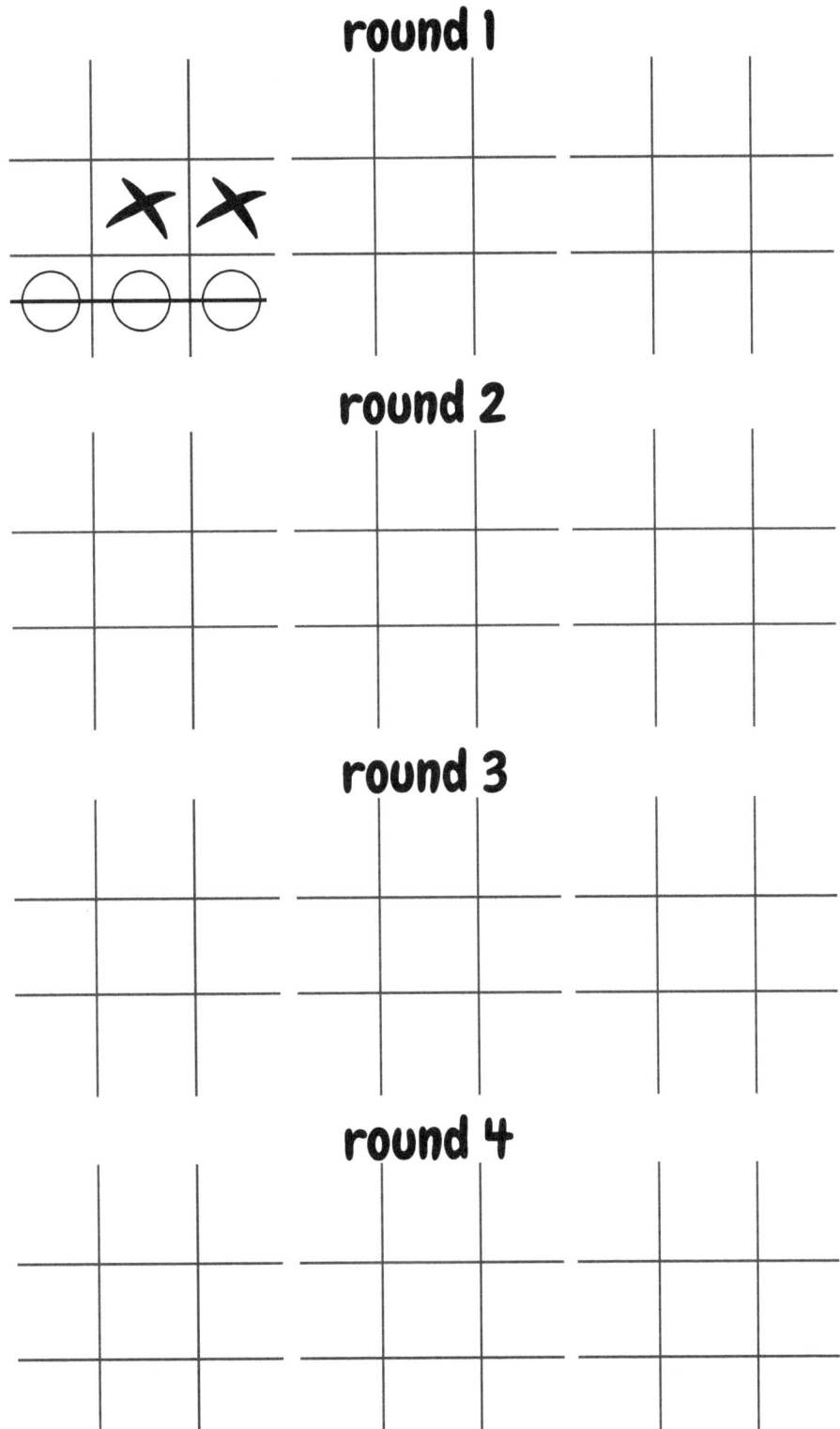

round 2

round 3

round 4

FUN AT SCHOOL

In the box, draw and color your favorite thing about school.

In school, I like _____

_____

because _____

_____

LET'S GO TO THE GARDEN AND DRAW!

Instructions:
In this garden, you'll find lots of leaves. Choose one and copy it by drawing and coloring.
Have fun!

4 IN A ROW

Each turn each player puts a piece of his color inside a column and it will fall until it reaches the lowest available spot. The one who can put 4 pieces of the same color in a row horizontally, vertically or diagonally wins.

PLAYER 1 : _____

PLAYER 2 : _____

WHO WINS ? : _____

MISSING PARTS

Draw a line to the missing part.

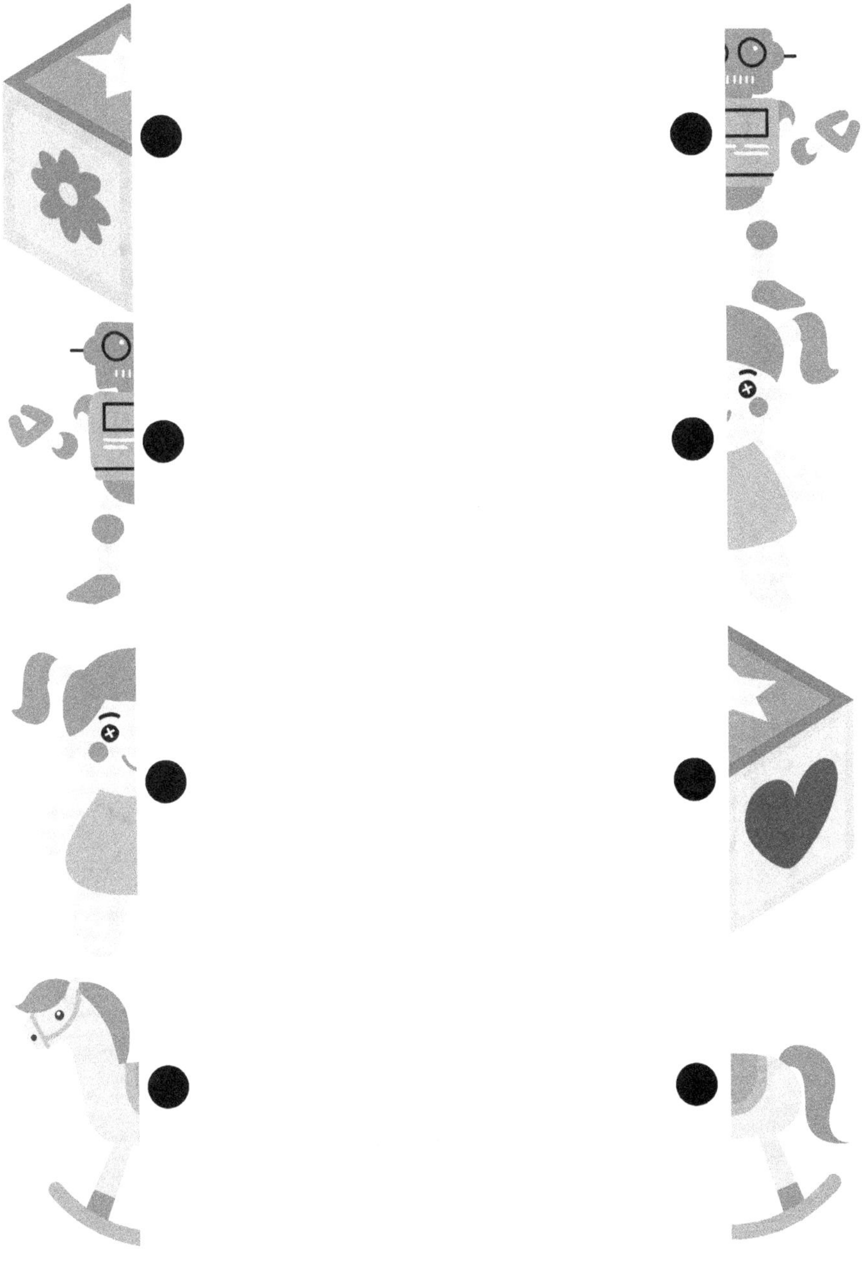

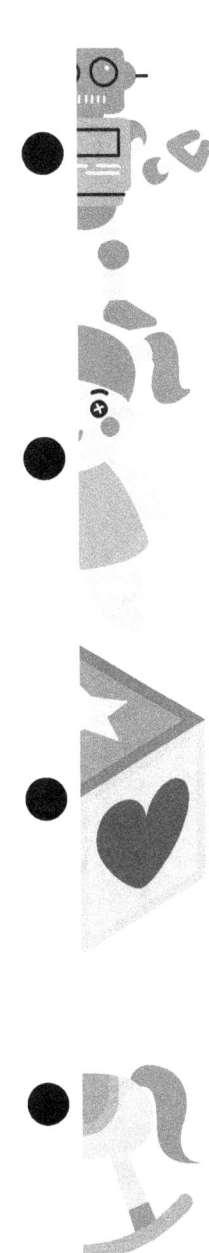
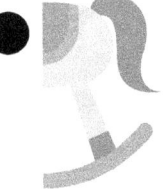

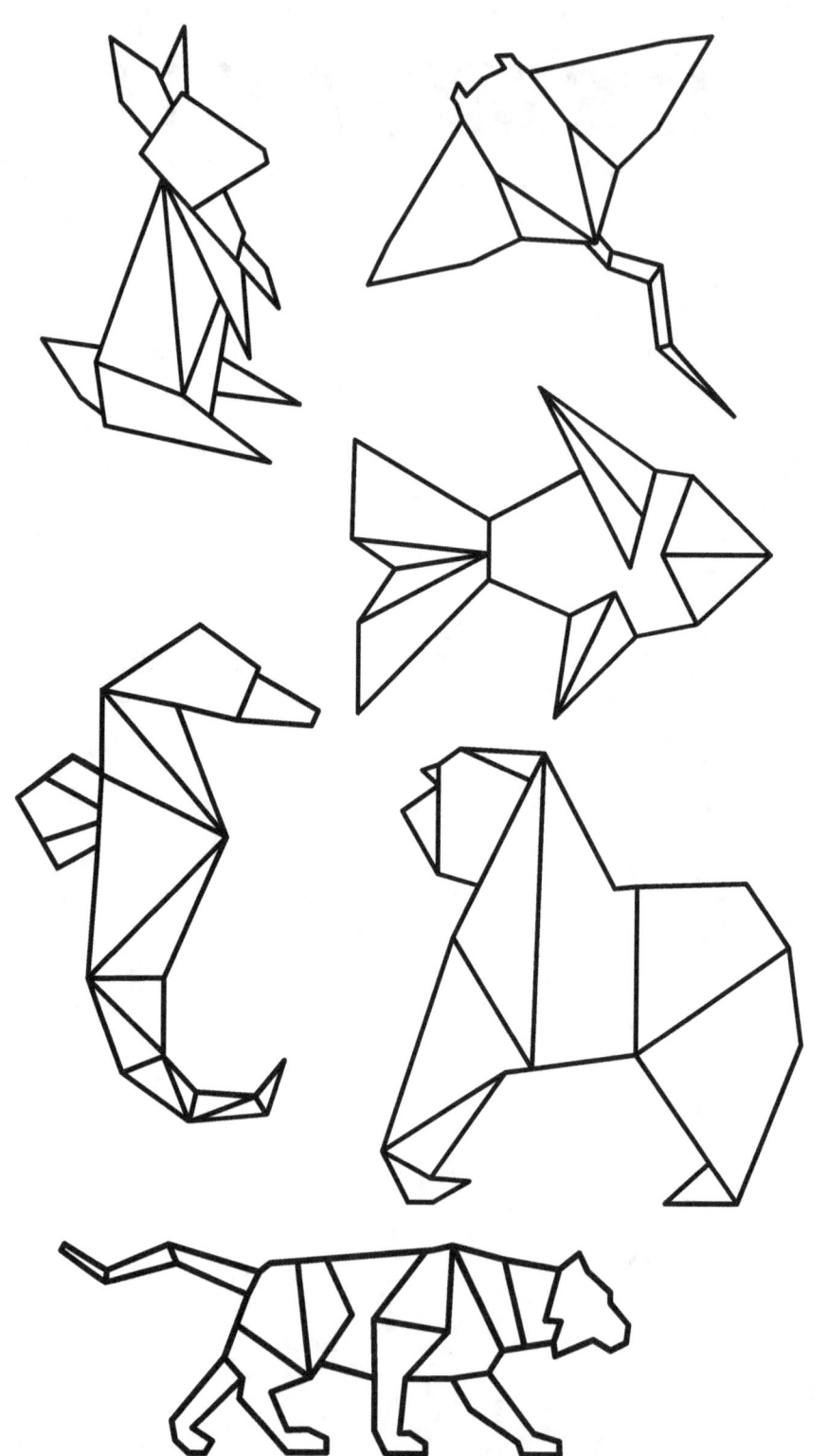

Mrs. Red's Fruit Stand

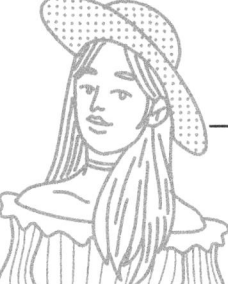

Mrs. Red sells fruit in boxes of **2**
Make sure each box has two by drawing the missing fruit.

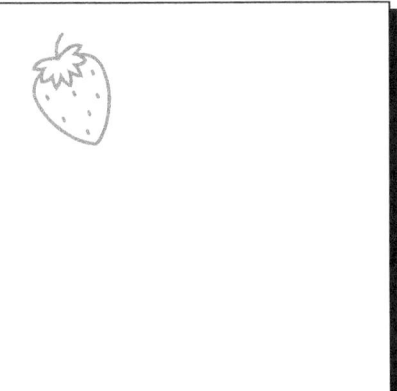

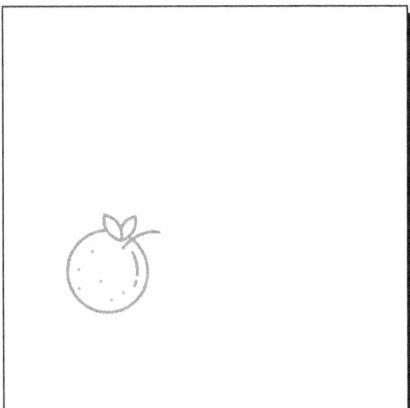

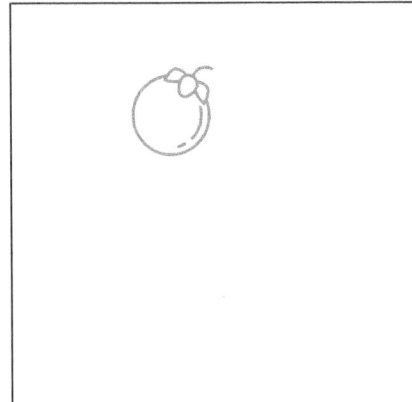

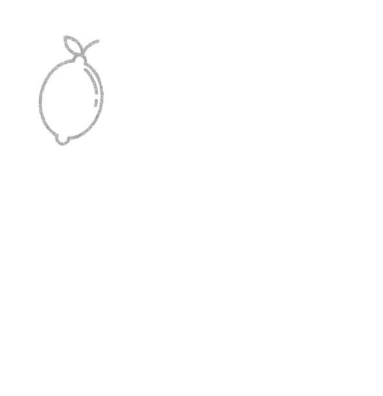

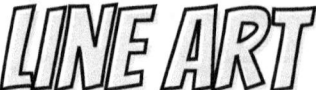

LINE ART

Demonstrate your mastery of geometric elements by creating an illustration using them! Use colored markers to identify them using the coloring key to the right.

COLORING KEY

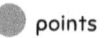 points

 rays

right angles

line segments

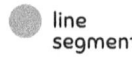 acute angles

obtuse angles

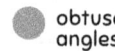 lines

MAZE !

Draw a line from start to exit.

start

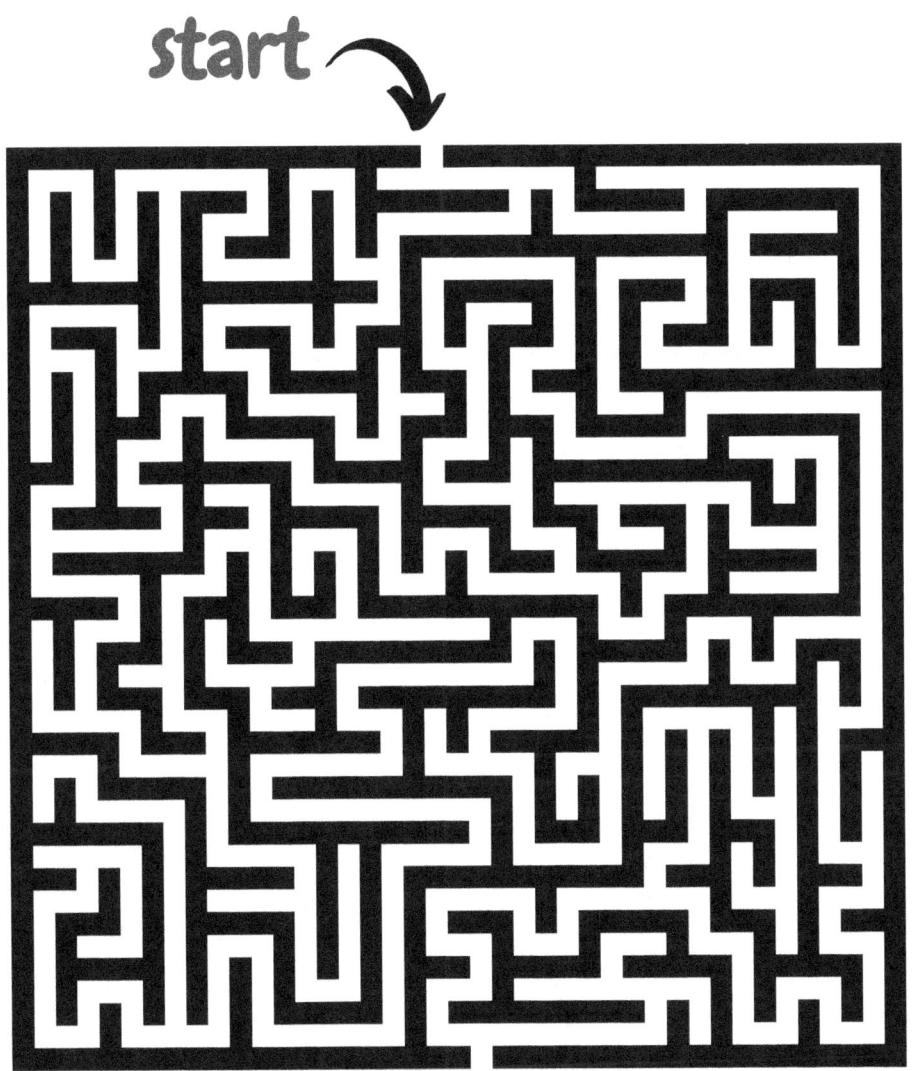

exit

LET'S GO TO THE GARDEN AND DRAW!

Instructions:
In this garden, you'll find many trees. Choose one and copy it by drawing and coloring.
Have fun!

FUN AT SCHOOL

In the box, draw and color your favorite thing about school.

In school, I like _____

_____

because _____

_____

_____

IT'S MONKEY TIME!

Help Monkey Set His Alarm

Instructions: Monkey follows a schedule for his daily tasks. Help him set his alarm by drawing the arms on the clock.

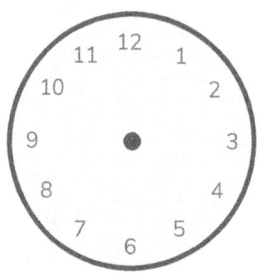

WAKE UP, MONKEY! 8:30AM

EAT LUNCH, MONKEY! 13:10AM

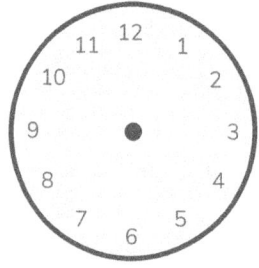

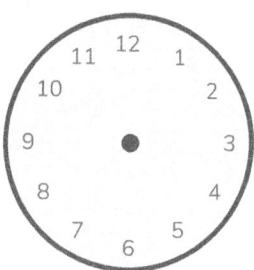

PLAY OUTSIDE, MONKEY! 3:50PM

GO TO BED, MONKEY! 8:30 PM

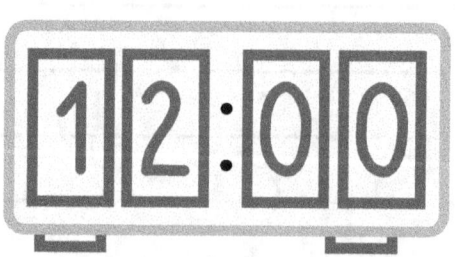

Mrs. Green's Fruit Stand

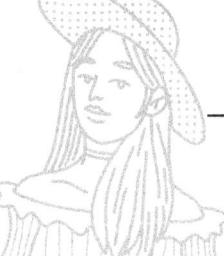

Mrs. Green sells fruit in boxes of **5**
Make sure each box has five by drawing the missing fruits.

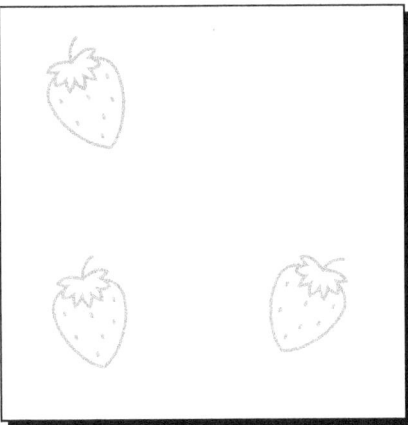

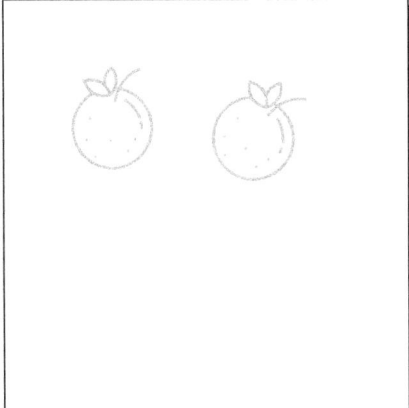

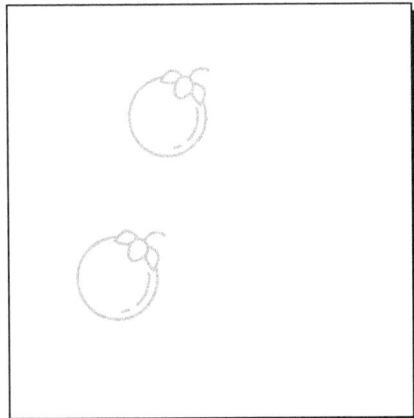

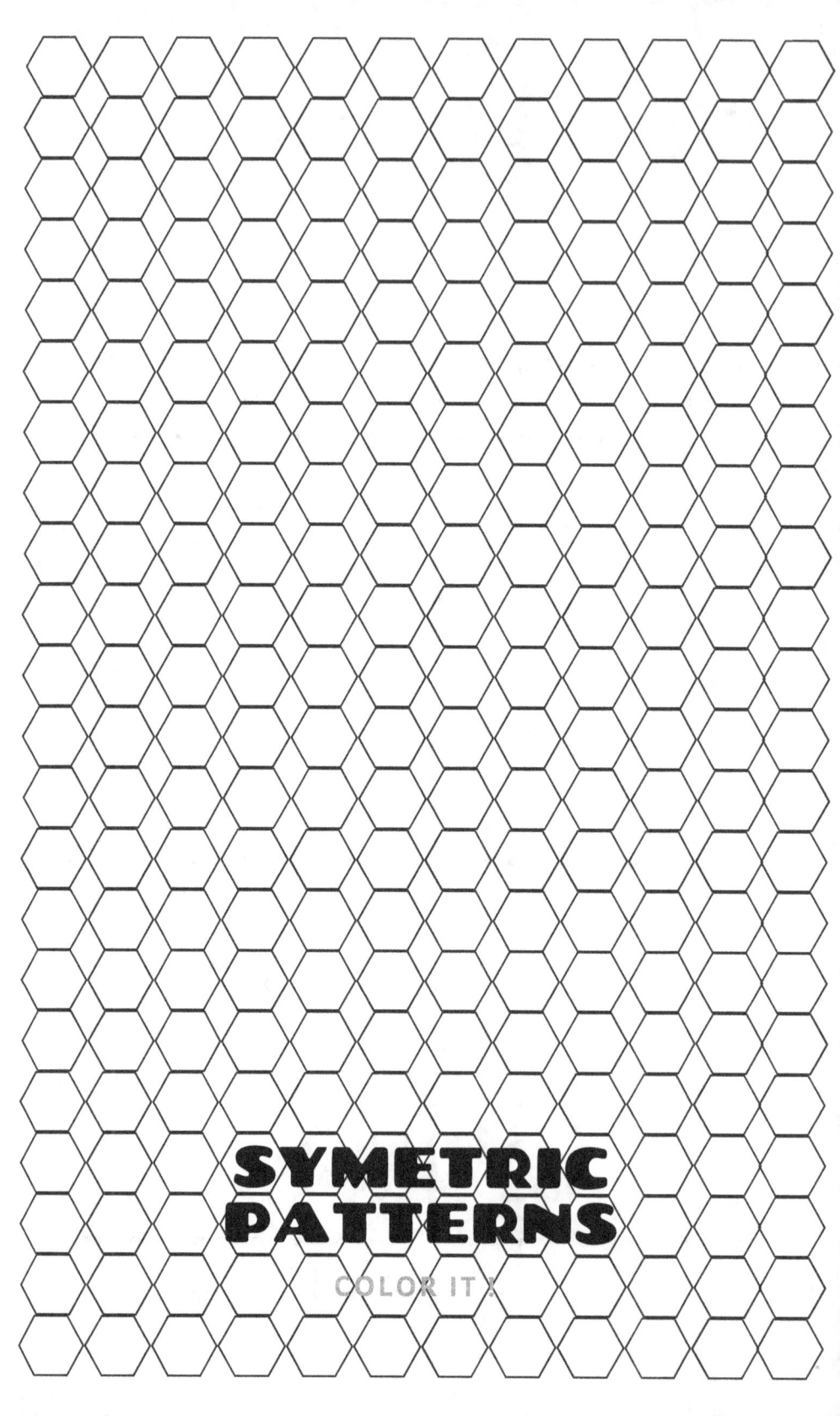

SYMETRIC
PATTERNS

COLOR IT !

POP ART GRID CHALLENGE

Print out 1 artwork by either Andy Warhol, Roy Lichtenstein, or Keith Haring. Draw a 5x5 grid on your photo. Using the materials you have, try to recreate the piece on the grid below by drawing one square at a time.

FUN WITH FRACTIONS

LEARN HOW TO ADD AND SUBTRACT FRACTIONS!

Write down the fraction indicated by each drawing in each row then write down the answer to the problem.

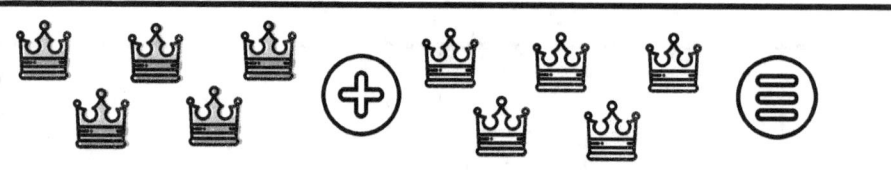

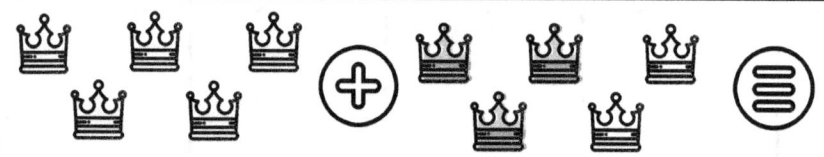

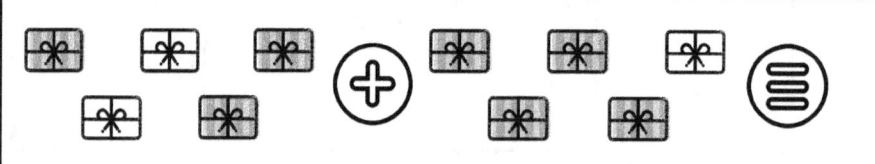

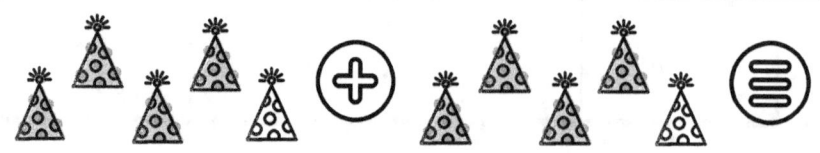

WHO IS SHE?

Use the space below to draw a portrait of your friend. On the left side, draw how she looks on the outside. On the right side, draw his favorite toys, animals, food, or games. Color your creation when you're done!

Materials:
Pencil, Crayons

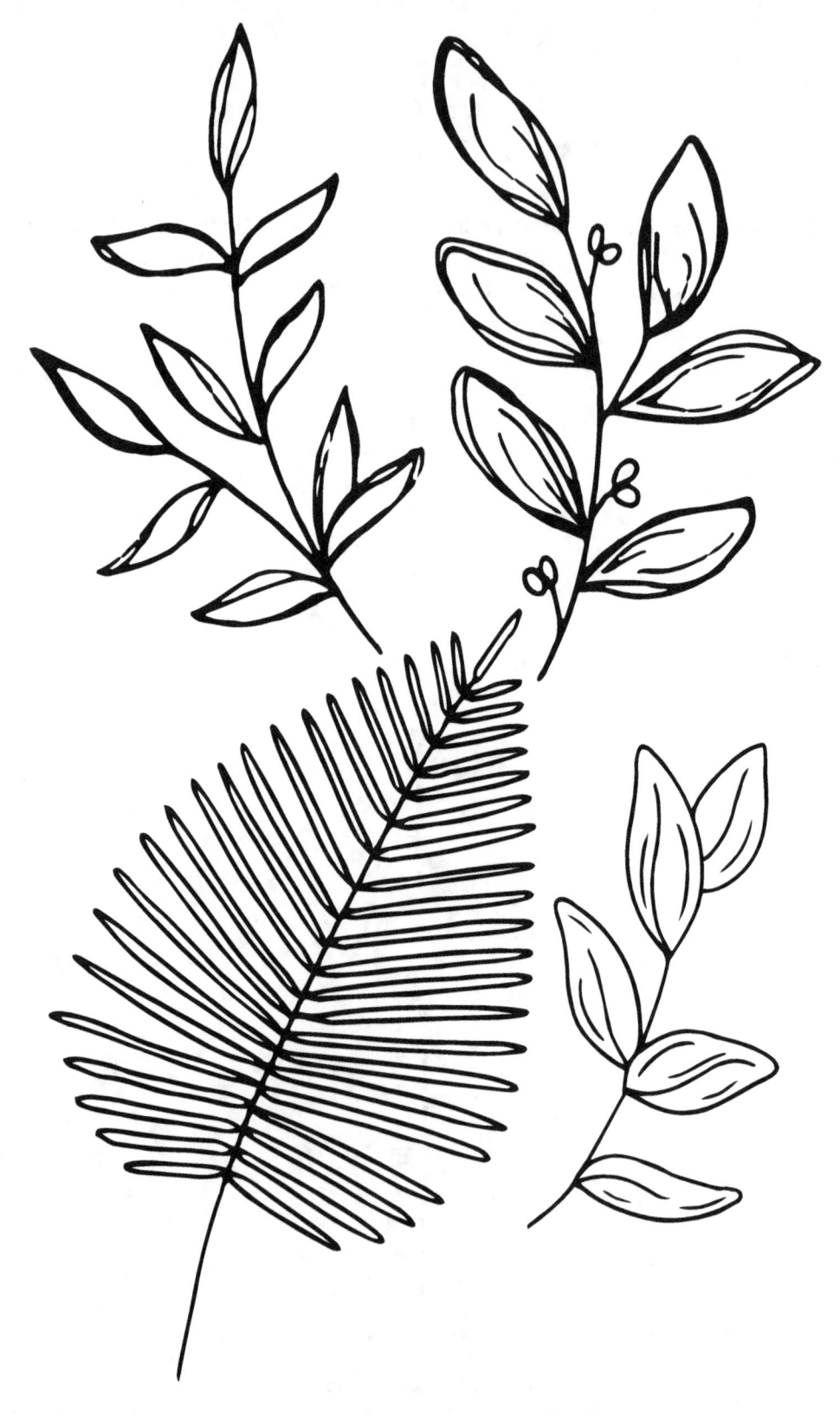

MISSING DOTS

Complete the equation by drawing the missing dots.

[dice: 3] + [ ] = 5   [dice: 4] + [ ] = 6

[ ] + [dice: 3] = 7   [ ] + [dice: 6] = 8

[dice: 1] + [ ] = 6   [dice: 3] + [ ] = 6

[ ] + [dice: 3] = 4   [ ] + [dice: 5] = 9

[dice: 1] + [ ] = 7   [dice: 4] + [ ] = 10

[ ] + [dice: 1] = 2   [ ] + [dice: 3] = 7

Mrs. Red's Fruit Stand

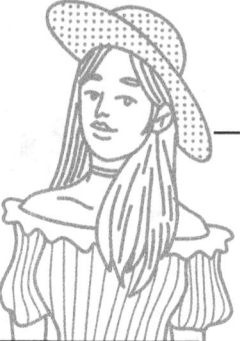

9

Mrs. Red sells fruit in boxes of
Make sure each box has nine by drawing the missing fruits.

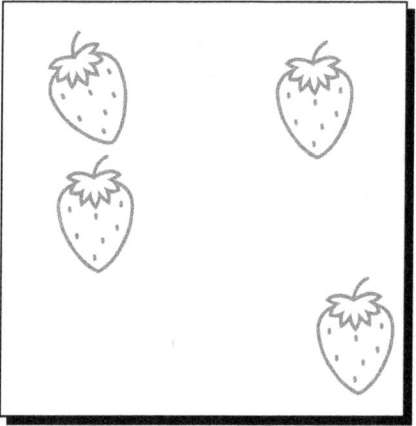

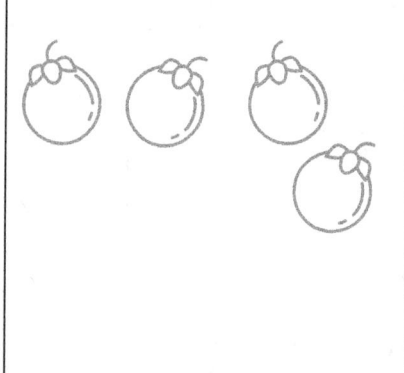

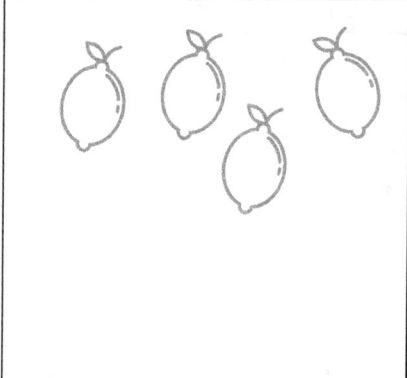

DRAW THE SHAPES

Continue drawing the shapes below.

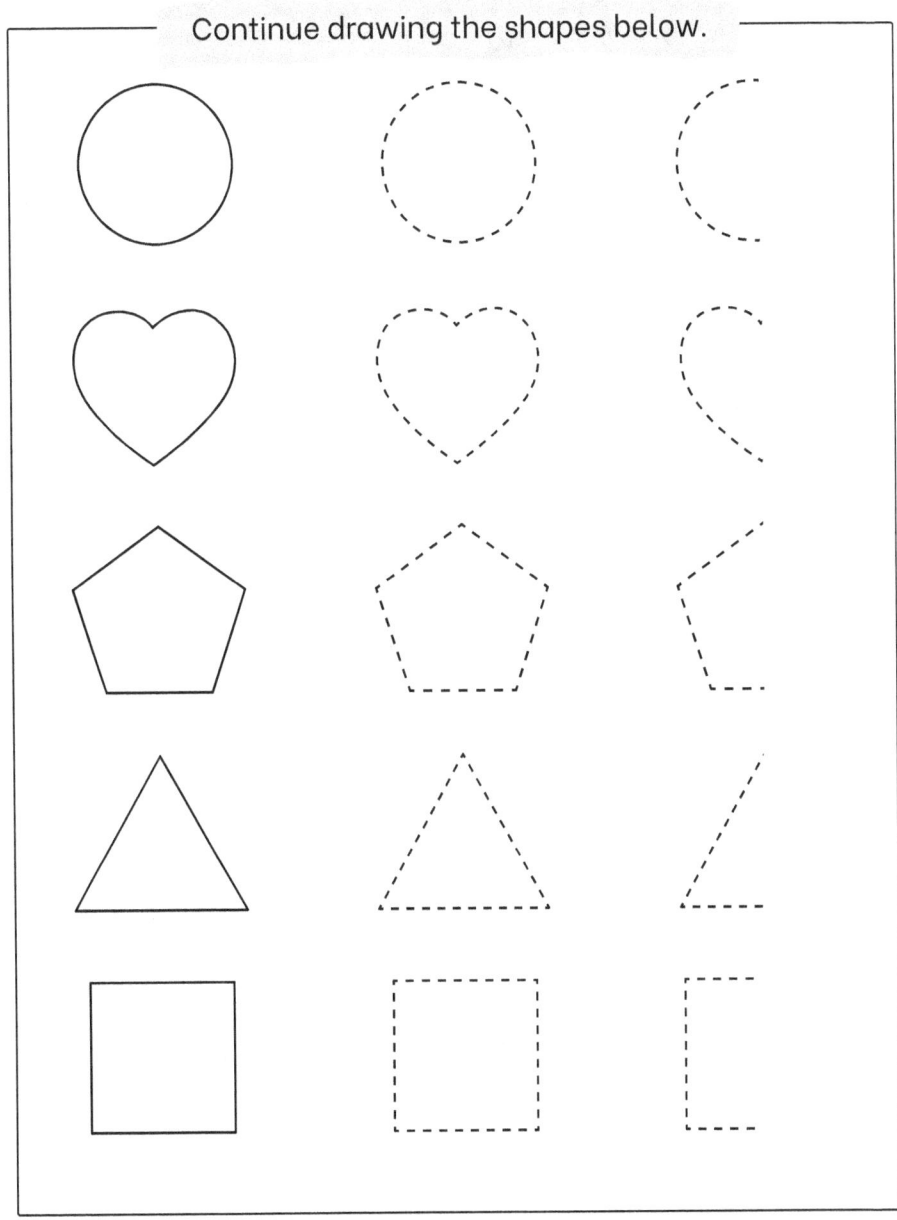

MAZE !

Draw a line from start to exit.

start

exit

4 IN A ROW

Each turn each player puts a piece of his color inside a column and it will fall until it reaches the lowest available spot.
The one who can put 4 pieces of the same color in a row horizontally, vertically or diagonally wins.

PLAYER 1 : _____

PLAYER 2 : _____

WHO WINS ? : _____

DRAW THE FACES

Continue drawing the faces below.

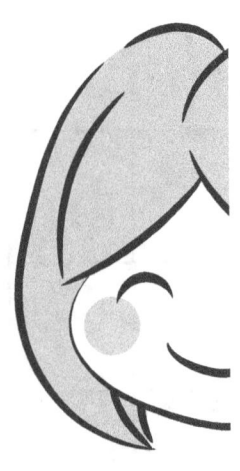

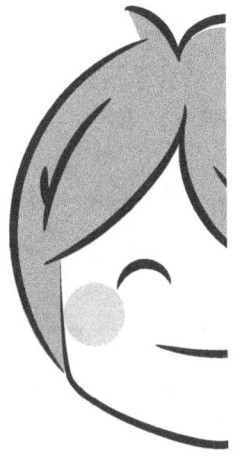

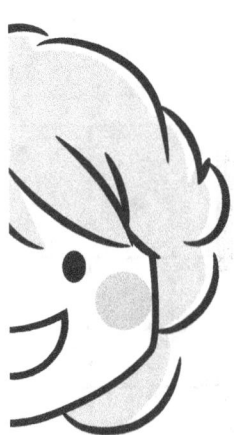

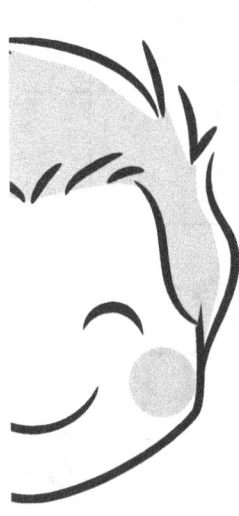

LINE ART

Demonstrate your mastery of geometric elements by creating an illustration using them! Use colored markers to identify them using the coloring key below.

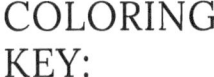 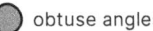
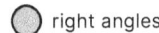

WHAT TIME IS IT?

Read the time from the digital clocks.
**Can you set the correct time on the analog
clocks by drawing the correct hands?**

5:15

8:30

8:00

7:55

Mrs. Green's Fruit Stand

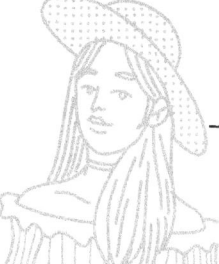

Mrs. Green sells fruit in boxes of **3**
Make sure each box has three by drawing the missing fruits.

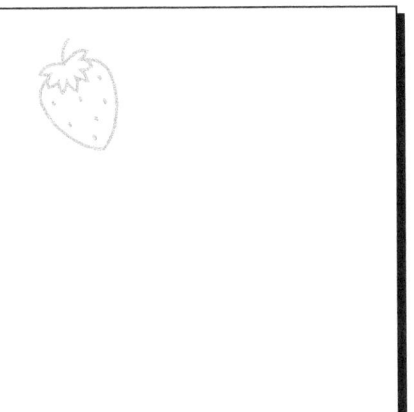

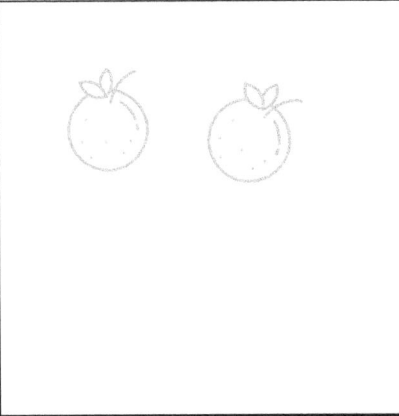

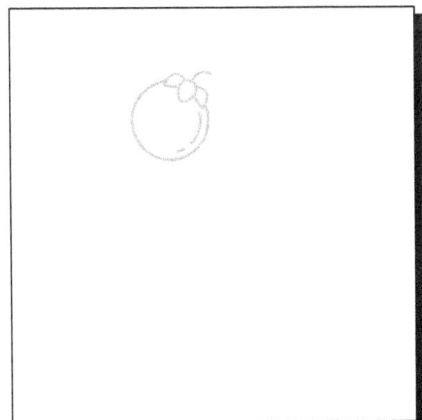

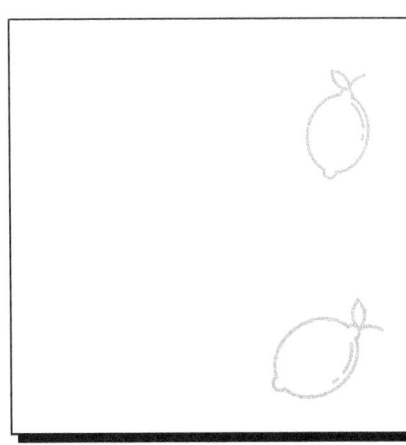

POP ART GRID CHALLENGE

Print out 1 artwork by either Andy Warhol, Roy Lichtenstein, or Keith Haring. Draw a 5x5 grid on your photo. Using the materials you have, try to recreate the piece on the grid below by drawing one square at a time.

IT'S MONKEY TIME!

Help Monkey Set His Alarm

Instructions: Monkey follows a schedule for his daily tasks.
Help him set his alarm by drawing the arms on the clock.

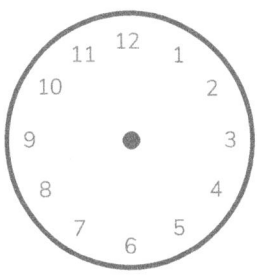

WAKE UP, MONKEY! 7:25 AM

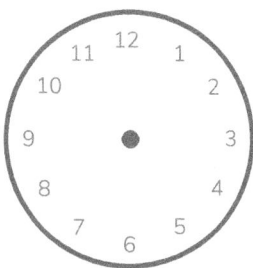

EAT LUNCH, MONKEY! 12:3 5AM

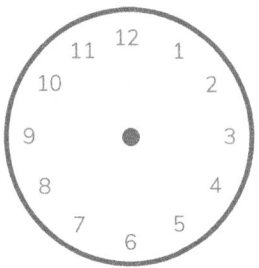

PLAY OUTSIDE, MONKEY! 5:10PM

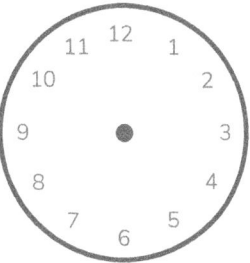

GO TO BED, MONKEY! 9:20 PM

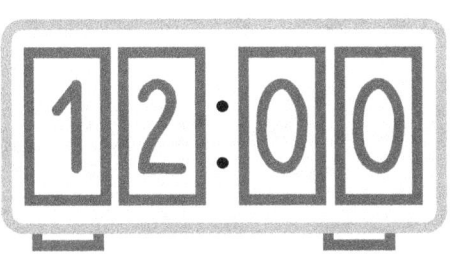

LINE ART

Demonstrate your mastery of geometric elements by creating an illustration using them! Use colored markers to identify them using the coloring key to the right.

COLORING KEY

- points
- rays
- right angles
- line segments
- acute angles
- obtuse angles
- lines

round 1

round 2

round 3

round 4

MISSING PARTS

Draw a line to the missing part.

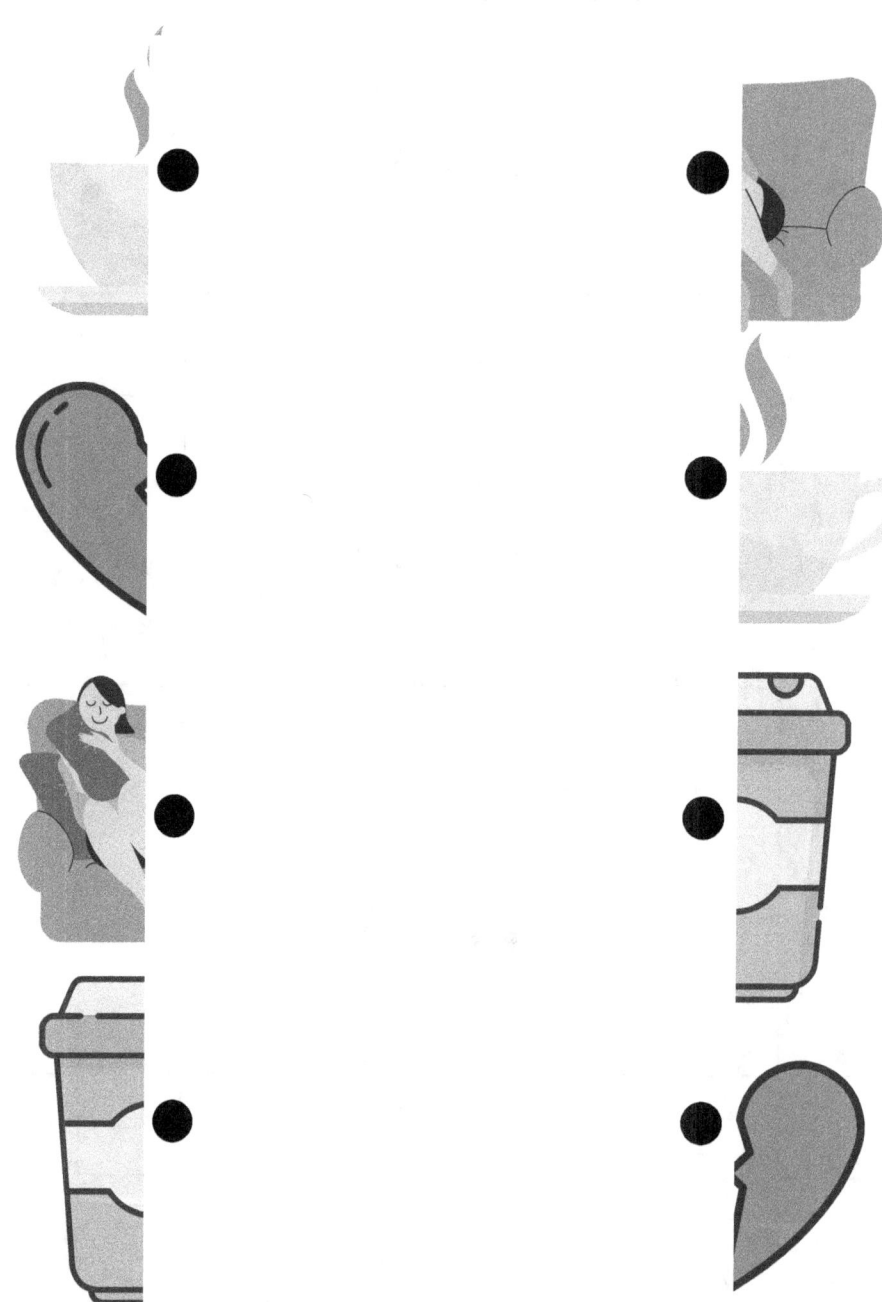

4 IN A ROW

Each turn each player puts a piece of his color inside a column and it will fall until it reaches the lowest available spot. The one who can put 4 pieces of the same color in a row horizontally, vertically or diagonally wins.

PLAYER 1 : _____

PLAYER 2 : _____

WHO WINS ? : _____

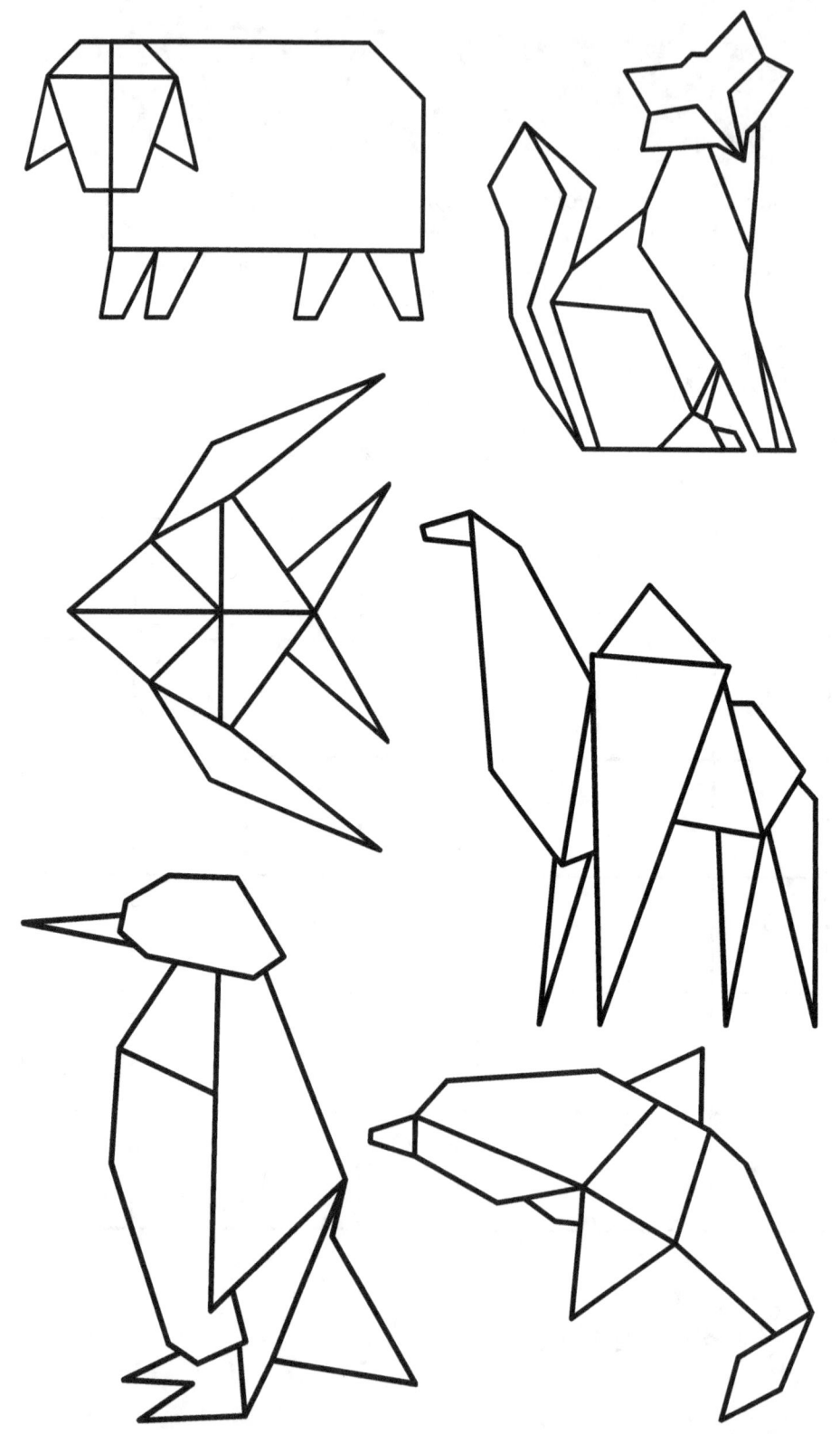

Mrs. Red's Fruit Stand

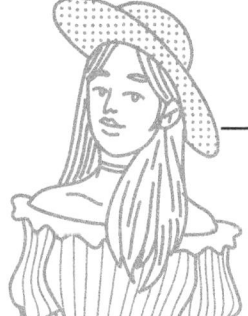

7

Mrs. Red sells fruit in boxes of
Make sure each box has seven by drawing the missing fruits.

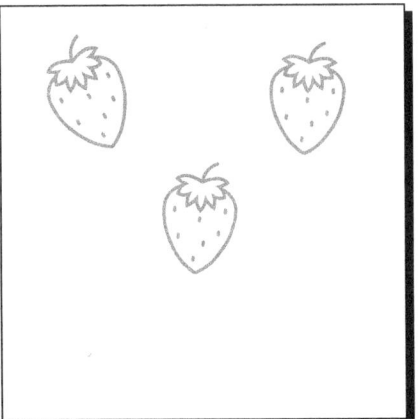

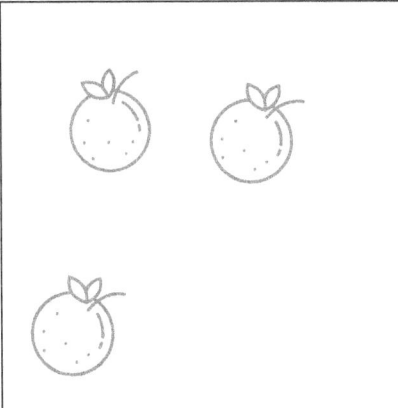

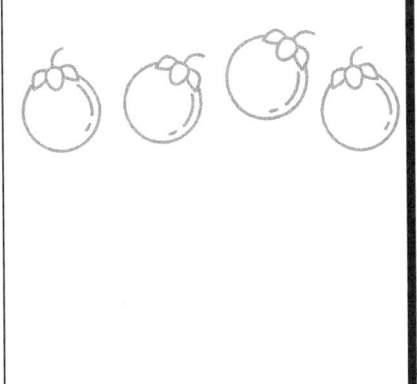

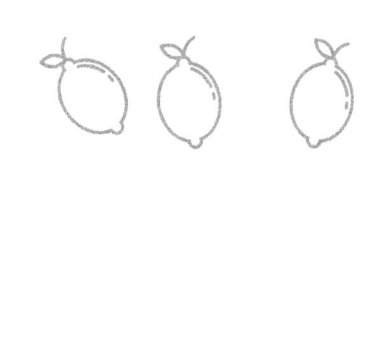

MAZE !

Draw a line from start to exit.

start

exit

FUN WITH FRACTIONS

LEARN HOW TO ADD AND SUBTRACT FRACTIONS!

Write down the fraction indicated by each drawing in each row then write down the answer to the problem.

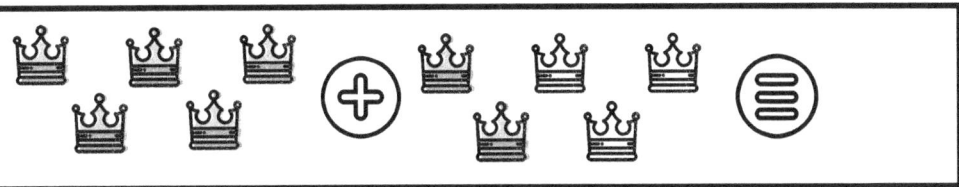

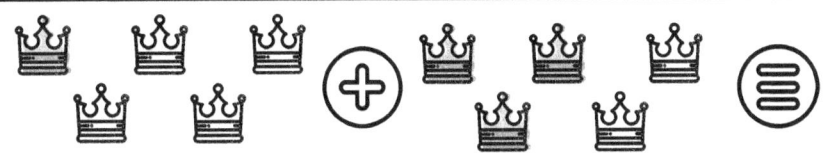

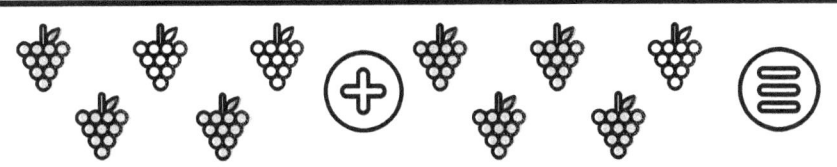

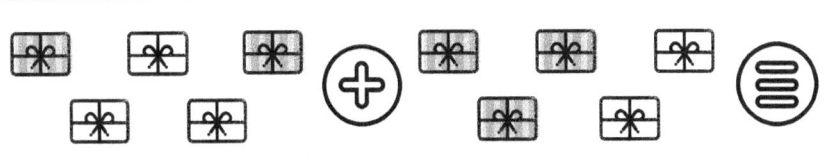

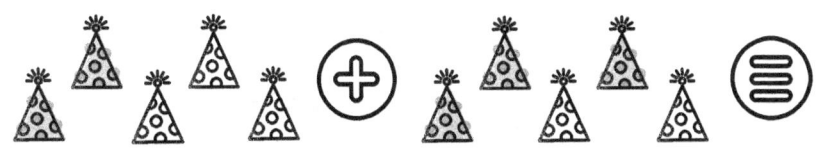

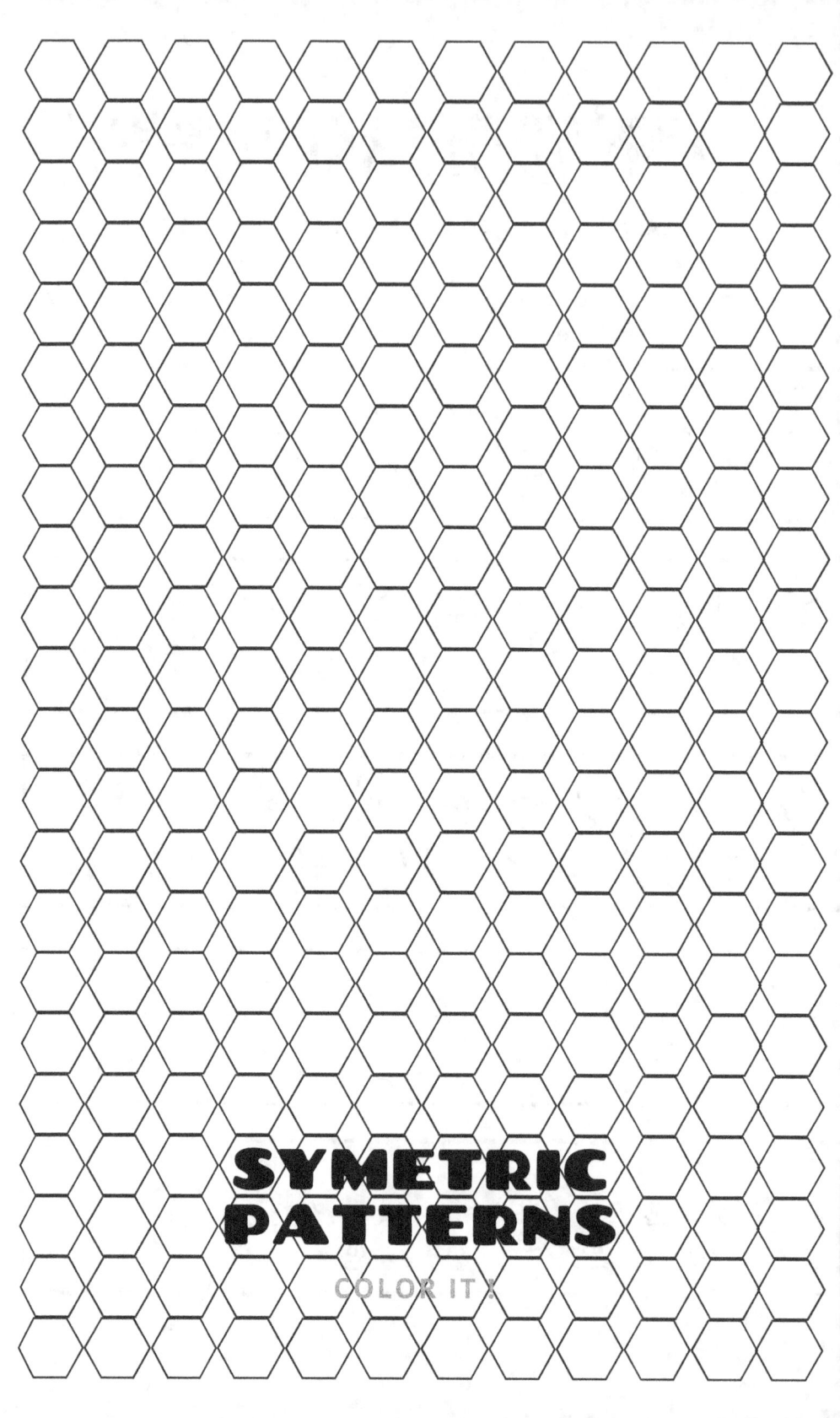

SYMETRIC
PATTERNS

COLOR IT X

www.ingramcontent.com/pod-product-compliance
Lightning Source LLC
Chambersburg PA
CBHW070614220526
45467CB00003B/1429